S0-AGM-150

WorldView 3

SERIES EDITOR: MICHAEL ROST

Terra Brockman

Longman

WorldView Workbook 3

Authorized adaptation from the United Kingdom edition entitled *Language to Go*, First Edition, published by Pearson Education Limited publishing under its Longman imprint. Copyright © 2002 by Pearson Education Limited

American English adaptation published by Pearson Education, Inc. Copyright © 2005.

Pearson Education, 10 Bank Street, White Plains, NY 10606

Editorial director: Pamela Fishman
Project manager: Irene Frankel
Senior development editors: Robin Longshaw, José Antonio Méndez
Vice president, director of design and production: Rhea Banker
Executive Managing editor: Linda Moser
Associate Managing editor: Mike Kemper
Production Editor: Sasha Kintzler
Art director: Elizabeth Carlson
Vice president, director of international marketing: Bruno Paul
Senior manufacturing buyer: Edie Pullman
Text and cover design: Elizabeth Carlson
Photo research: Aerin Csigay
Text composition: Word & Image Design
Text font: 9.5/13pt Frutiger Roman and 9/11pt Frutiger Bold

ISBN: 0-13-184010-X
Printed in the United States of America
4 5 6 7 8 9 10–CRS–09 08 07 06 05

Acknowledgments
Contributing writer Ellen Kisslinger, for her work on the Self-Quizzes.

Ilustration Credits
Steve Attoe, pages 4-11, 27, 29, 46, 57, 68, 82; John Etheridge, 70, 85, 92, 102; Dave MacKay, 60, 77, 96; Paul McCusker, 61, 65, 67, 74, 84; Grant Miehm, 89, 101, 104; Suzanne Mogensen, 13, 23, 96, 106; Steve Schulman, 15, 83; Neil Stewart, 30, 36, 61, 91; Gary Torrisi, 50, 58, 99.

Photo credits
Page 26, Peter Cade/Getty Images; 32, (left) Tony Arruza/Getty Images, (right) Larry Gatz/Getty Images; 34, David Sacks/Getty Images; 35, Kevin Peterson/Getty Images; 37, Image State/AGE Fotostock; 40, David Sutherland/Getty Images; 43, Ray Massey/Getty Images; 44, Michael Keller/Corbis; 51, Trevor Clifford; 56, (left) Corbis Stock Market/Paul Barton, (right) Corbis Stock Market/Larry Williams; 63, (1) Michael Keller/Corbis, (2) Thomas Del Brase/Getty Images, (3) Getty Images, (4) Corbis Images/PictureQuest, (5) Zefa Visual Media - Germany/Index Stock Imagery, (6) Howard Huang/Getty Images; 71, Royalty-Free/Corbis; 73, (A) Chinch Gryniewicz/ Ecoscene/ Corbis, (B) Junko Kimura/Getty Images, (C) Siede Preis/Getty Images, (D) Terry Mccormick/Getty Images; 75, Doug Mazell/Index Stock Imagery; 76, Trevor Clifford; 78, (left) C Squared Studios/Getty Images, (middle left) Kevin Peterson/Getty Images, (middle right) Barbara Penoyar/Getty Images, (right) Kevin Peterson/Getty Images; 79, Digital Vision/Getty Images; 88, Royalty-Free/Corbis; 90, Gareth Boden; 106, Kevin Peterson/Getty Images.

Contents

Learning Strategies

Here are 6 ways to improve your listening.

Check (✓) the strategies that you use now. Try a new strategy each week. In the column on the right, write the date you tried it and take notes about your experience. Did the strategy help you learn?

1 ☐ **Find new sources**

What do you like to listen to or watch in English? Movies? Songs? News broadcasts? TV shows? The radio? Interviews? Conversations? Find some new sources for listening. You can use the radio, TV, CDs, DVDs, the Internet, your computer lab, or visit some places where you can hear people speak English. Listen at least one hour a week.

Try this now:

What do you like to listen to in English? (songs, movies, etc.) Write two or three ideas.

What are your favorite sources for listening to English? (CDs, Internet, etc.) Write two or three sources.

Date: _____
Notes: _____
_____
_____
_____
_____
_____
_____

2 ☐ **Predict words and ideas**

What do you already know? Before you listen to something, think about the topic, the ideas, and the people speaking. Can you predict some of the content? (Before you listen, say or write three words and two ideas you might hear.)

Try this now:

Look at the photographs on pages 30 and 31 of your *WorldView Student Book*. What are the speakers talking about? What words will they use?

Date: _____
Notes: _____
_____
_____
_____
_____
_____
_____

3 ☐ **Listen for a specific purpose**

When you listen, you don't need to understand everything. Listen for a specific purpose. What information do you want to find out? Names, numbers, important events, key information, the speaker's feelings, or the main idea?

Try this now:

Think about some different listening situations. What listening purpose would you have in each of these?

• You're at an airport. There's an announcement.
• You're driving in your car. There's a song on the radio.
• You're at home. There's a news show on TV.

Date: _____
Notes: _____
_____
_____
_____
_____
_____
_____

4 ☐ Use key words and images

When we listen, we can often understand the main idea from key words and images. "Key words" are the important words. "Key images" are actions and emotions that the speakers use. When you listen, pick out a few key words and images.

Try this now:

Choose a scene from a movie or video. (Most scenes are about three minutes long.) Watch the scene and write down a few key words and images. Look at your list. What is the main idea of the scene?

Date: _____

Notes: _____

_____

_____

_____

_____

_____

5 ☐ Use dictation for intensive listening

Dictation can help you focus on grammar and vocabulary when you listen. Choose a short (30-second) conversation from a video or audio. Play it one time and just listen to get the meaning. Then listen again. Press "pause" after each sentence. Write exactly what you hear.

Try this now:

Here are some ideas to use for dictation. Which ones do you like? Write a plus (+) sign.

_____ write every word
_____ write in your own words
_____ write only the verbs (or nouns)

Date: _____

Notes: _____

_____

_____

_____

_____

_____

6 ☐ Keep a listening notebook

Write notes about your listening experiences. After you listen to a news broadcast or watch a movie, write for two minutes in your listening notebook. Write a summary or a reaction or some new vocabulary or expressions. Write in your notebook once or twice a week.

Try this now:

Think about some ideas for your listening notebook. Which might be helpful for you to write? Write a plus (+) sign.

_____ a summary   _____ new expressions
_____ questions   _____ your impressions
_____ other notes

Date: _____

Notes: _____

_____

_____

_____

_____

_____

Learning Strategies

Vocabulary Strategies

Here are 6 ways to improve your vocabulary.

Check (✓) the strategies that you use now. Try a new strategy each week. In the column on the right, write the date you tried it and take notes about your experience. Did the strategy help you learn?

1 ☐ **Add "shared" words to your vocabulary**

What English words are similar in your language? For example *optimist* in English and *optimista* in Spanish are very similar. Think of "shared" words between English and your language. (Most languages have hundreds of shared words.)

Try this now:

How do you say these English words in your language? Which ones are shared words in English? Do they have the same meaning?

color   data   favor   information   tourist

What other shared words do you know?

Date: _____

Notes: _____

_____

_____

_____

_____

_____

_____

2 ☐ **Make word cards to learn new vocabulary**

On a small card, write a new word or expression on one side. On the other side, draw a picture of the word, write a short definition of the word, or write a sentence with the word. For example, write *bride* on one side of the card and draw a picture on the other side. Make 3–5 new cards each day. Review these cards for a few minutes, once or twice a week.

Try this now:

Think about how you learn new vocabulary. How many new words or expressions can you learn well in one week?

____ fewer than 5   ____ between 5 and 10
____ between 11 and 20   ____ more than 20

Date: _____

Notes: _____

_____

_____

_____

_____

_____

3 ☐ **Make word webs**

Make word webs to show how words are related. Each line is a new link for the word.

Make one word web each week in a vocabulary notebook. Save your word webs. Review them and add new words to them.

Try this now:

Make a word web for two of these words. Add about 5 links for each one.

throw away   messy   backache   get off   awful

Date: _____

Notes: _____

_____

_____

_____

_____

_____

4 ☐ **Narrate in English**

Look around you or watch a video with no sound. As you look, say what you see in English. You can say the names of objects (for example, *a tree, a red car, a man with a hat, a clear blue sky*) or you can describe actions (for example, *a child is talking to her mother*). Say at least 10 things. Try this once a week for 5 minutes.

Try this now:

Look around you. Name at least 10 things you see, in English. Then say something about each thing. (Example: *My cell phone also works as a digital camera.*) Does this help you to "think in English"?

Date: _____

Notes: _____

_____

_____

_____

_____

_____

5 ☐ **Use a memory technique**

Use a memory technique to help you remember new words. One method is the "key word method." It is a way of mixing sounds and images. For a new word, think of an image, using ideas from your language or from English. For example, an *executive* is a *businessperson who makes decisions for a business*. The first part of the word sounds like *eggs* and the third part sounds like *cute*, so you might picture a businessman at a desk with three "cute" eggs above his head. He is trying to decide which one to choose. This mixed image may help you remember the new word.

Try this now:

Think about memory techniques you use. Find the meaning of these English words and try to memorize them using the "key word method" or another memory technique.

nutritious   *politics*   *can't stand*

Date: _____

Notes: _____

_____

_____

_____

_____

6 ☐ **Read for pleasure**

Use popular books or Penguin readers (available from Longman). Find a book that is comfortable for you to read. (*Comfortable* means that you can understand about 90% of the words.) Read every day for 20 minutes or more. Don't use a dictionary. Guess the meaning of new words from their context.

Try this now:

Think about what you like to read. What topics are most interesting for you to read about? Put these topics in order of interest (1–9) for you: 1 = most interesting.

____ famous people   ____ mystery   ____ sports
____ adventure   ____ romance   ____ politics
____ history   ____ travel   ____ science fiction

Date: _____

Notes: _____

_____

_____

_____

_____

_____

Learning Strategies

Grammar Strategies

Here are 6 ways to improve your grammar.

Check (✓) the strategies that you use now. Try a new strategy each week. In the column on the right, write the date you tried it and take notes about your experience. Did the strategy help you learn?

1 ☐ **Get feedback from a conversation partner**

Find a conversation partner. Meet at least once a week for 30 minutes. Speak English only. Does your partner understand you? Does your partner correct your grammar? Make a note of any grammar mistakes that your conversation partner (or your English teacher or classmates) notices.

Try this now:

Think about how you practice English outside of class. Do you have an English conversation partner? If "yes," how often do you meet to speak in English? If you don't have a partner, can you find one? Can you and a classmate be conversation partners?

Date: _____

Notes: _____

_____

_____

_____

_____

_____

2 ☐ **Say it in different words**

Look at a newspaper, magazine, or book. Find three sentences with difficult grammar. Say them or write them in different words.

Try this now:

Say or write each of these sentences in other words.

1. Boys are not as organized as girls. (Hint: Use *more organized*.)
2. We were able to speak English when we were young. (Hint: Use *could*.)
3. The cheese is made fresh every day. (Hint: Use *make*.)

Date: _____

Notes: _____

_____

_____

_____

_____

_____

3 ☐ **Imagine the conversation**

Find a photograph (in a magazine or book) of two or more people talking. Imagine the conversation. What are they saying? Write down at least four lines of their conversation. A few days later, go back and double-check your grammar.

Try this now:

Look at page 107 in your *WorldView Student Book*. Imagine the conversation for the picture. Write down at least four lines.

Date: _____

Notes: _____

_____

_____

_____

_____

_____

4 ☐ **Do a grammar search**

Choose a grammar point from the *WorldView Student Book* that you want to study, such as a verb tense (like the past passive) or a structure (like *so, too, either,* or *not either*).

Look through a newspaper (articles, comics, etc.), or a magazine (interviews, articles, etc.), or a book (a novel, a biography, etc.). Look for five examples of the grammar point you are studying. Circle the examples. Write the example phrases or sentences in your notebook.

Try this now:

Write three grammar points that you would you like to work on:

_____ _____ _____

Date: _____

Notes: _____

_____

_____

_____

_____

5 ☐ **Play it back**

Choose a topic to talk about in English, such as your job or a favorite movie. Plan for a few minutes: What will you say? Write notes (not sentences!) on a card. Now record your speech (don't look at your card). Talk for one minute. Play back your speech. Write down exactly what you said. Look at the transcript. What parts can you improve by changing the grammar?

Try this now:

Imagine you are giving a speech to your class. Here are some examples of topics for a short speech. Check (✓) the one you want to talk about or add another.

____ my favorite vacation place
____ my best friend
____ another topic: _____

Date: _____

Notes: _____

_____

_____

_____

_____

_____

6 ☐ **Keep a journal**

Write freely in English for five minutes about anything you want. Let your ideas flow and don't edit what you write—just write. Write two or three times a week for five minutes each time. Choose a new topic each time.

Try this now:

Here are some examples of topics you can write about. Check three topics that you want to write about in English.

____ A typical day for me
____ A habit I want to change
____ My likes and dislikes
____ An interesting person I know
____ My first impression of (a present/a place)

Date: _____

Notes: _____

_____

_____

_____

_____

_____

Learning Strategies

Pronunciation Strategies

Here are 6 ways to improve your pronunciation.

Check (✓) the strategies that you use now. Try a new strategy each week. In the column on the right, write the date you tried it and take notes about your experience. Did the strategy help you learn?

1 ☐ **Make a list of target phrases**

Make a list of target phrases. These are the phrases that have difficult words and sounds for you. Put these on notes and post them around your home. Practice saying your target phrases every day—loudly, clearly, and confidently.

Try this now:

Which of these phrases contain sounds that are difficult for you to pronounce?

*a few drops of olive oil   six sticks of butter
a chunk of cheese*

What other English sounds, names, words, or phrases are difficult for you to pronounce? Make a list.

Date: _____

Notes: _____

_____

_____

_____

_____

_____

_____

_____

2 ☐ **Shadow what you hear**

Listen to a recorded conversation, such as a conversation on your *WorldView* CD. Use the pause button on the CD player. Pause after each turn in the conversation. Repeat exactly what the speaker says (*shadow*) or repeat the last part of what the speaker says (*echo*). Don't think too much; just try to keep shadowing. Do this for just two minutes a day.

Try this now:

Think of three specific sources you can use for shadowing. _____ _____ _____

Date: _____

Notes: _____

_____

_____

_____

_____

_____

_____

_____

3 ☐ **Say it with emotion**

Practice using emotions to stretch your voice in English. Pick some simple sentences and say them in different ways—imagine that you are in different situations or in different emotional states. How is your voice different for each one?

Try this now:

Say these two sentences with three different emotions.

Let's go home now.   What time is it?

Here are some emotions:

friendly   angry   confused   happy   worried

Date: _____

Notes: _____

_____

_____

_____

_____

_____

4 ☐ **Mark the rhythm**

Choose a line from a conversation on your *WorldView* CD or from another audio or video recording. Close your eyes. Pay attention to the rhythm. The rhythm of English is the pattern of stressed (long and clear) and unstressed (short and weak) syllables and the chunking of words into groups.

Write down the line of conversation and mark the text. Place a slash mark (/) at each pause—this is a "chunk." Underline or draw a circle over the strongest words in each chunk—this is the stress.

Try this now:

Say the sentence below to yourself. Stress the words that are bold and make the other words short and weak.

What *do you* ***do*** */ on the* ***week****end?*

Date: _____
Notes: _____
_____
_____
_____
_____
_____

5 ☐ **Speak in phrases**

When fluent speakers speak English, they connect words, and the sounds in the words often change. There are many phrases in English that have linked sounds, such as *wanna* for *want to* and *gonna* for *going to.*

Try this now:

The underlined spellings here show how the phrases are pronounced. First, rewrite the phrase with its normal spelling. Then pronounce it with the linked sounds.

Howzit going?	*Howja* like the movie?
Whaddaya think?	*Whatser* name?
C'mon. Hurry up.	*Seeya* later.
I *hafta* go home.	I *wanna* talk to you.
I've *gotta* go.	*G'won.* I'll be there in a minute.

What other phrases with linked sounds do you know?

Date: _____
Notes: _____
_____
_____
_____
_____
_____

6 ☐ **Find your own voice**

Choose a story, like a children's story or part of a novel. Record yourself on audio or video three times. Each time, set a goal to improve one specific area of your pronunciation: loudness and clarity, chunking (saying words in groups), prominence (stressing the most important word in each chunk), intonation (making your pitch rise and fall clearly), or individual sounds. Listen to your recording. Note where you have improved.

Try this now:

Think about some stories or books in English that you can read aloud from. What are two you can use to make a recording (a specific story or part of a story)?

_____ _____

Date: _____
Notes: _____
_____
_____
_____
_____
_____

Nice to see you again

Vocabulary

1 Match the sentences to the correct function.

A. Greeting	**B.** Introducing	**C.** Complimenting
D. Making conversation	**E.** Ending a conversation	

1. The weather has been really wonderful. _D_

2. That's a great scarf! _____

3. I'd like you to meet my friend Nadia. _____

4. This is my husband, Martin. _____

5. Goodbye. _____

6. That was a fun party. _____

7. Hi, Doug, how's it going? _____

8. See you later. _____

9. Hello, Maria. How are you doing? _____

10. Did you watch the show about Alaska last night? _____

2 Unscramble the words to make sentences.

1. have / for / coffee? / Do / time / you
   _Do you have time for coffee?_____

2. tie. / that's / Hey, / great / a
   _____

3. you / OK, / later. / see
   _____

4. everything / fine. / I'm / but / is / busy,
   _____

5. you / are / Nelson, / Hi, / how / doing?
   _____

6. a / wife. / present / Thanks. / was / It / my / from
   _____

7. appointment. / for / late / an / Sorry, / I'm / but
   _____

8. goodbye. / OK,
   _____

3 Put the sentences from Exercise 2 in the correct order to make a conversation.

A: _Hi, Nelson, how are you doing?_____

B: _____

A: _____

B: _____

A: _____

B: _____

A: _____

B: _____

Grammar

4 Look at the pictures. What do Henry and Hiroko usually do? What are they doing these days? Underline the correct form of the verb.

Henry and Hiroko are farmers. They **1.** (live / are living) in Illinois. They usually **2.** (work / are working) outdoors. They **3.** (grow / are growing) vegetables and **4.** (raise / are raising) chickens for eggs. Hiroko and Henry **5.** (think / are thinking) about buying a new car because the one they have **6.** (gets / is getting) old, but they **7.** (wait / are waiting) for a good deal.

But these days Hiroko and Henry **8.** (don't think / are not thinking) about those problems because they **9.** (plan / are planning) their vacation. They **10.** (think / are thinking) about going to Japan. They **11.** (go / are going) there every year because they always **12.** (have / are having) a great time with friends and relatives. They can't wait to leave.

5 Use the correct form of the verb in the simple present or present continuous to complete Elizabeth's email to her friend Julia.

To: Julia
From: Elizabeth

Hi Julia. How <u>are you doing</u>? I _____ much to do today, and I'm also kind of depressed
1. (you do)   2. (not have)

because Tom called me this morning to say that he can't see me tonight. I think he _____ too
                                                                              3. (work)

hard these days. He _____ to make more money, so he usually _____ until very late.
                    4. (want)   5. (work)

On top of that, he _____ French classes this semester because he _____ to France on
                   6. (take)   7. (go)

business often. In case that's not enough, he _____ his apartment and he _____
                                              8. (paint)   9. (help)

his mother with some renovations in her house. The truth is, he _____ a minute for me, and I
                                                                10. (not have)

_____ to feel lonely.
11. (begin)

Anyway, if you _____ plans, maybe we can watch a movie or go out to dinner.
               12. (not have)

Let me know if you are free tonight.

See you,

Liz

Listening

6 ∩ Play track 2. Listen to the conversation. Put the topics and functions of the conversation in the correct order.

_____ talk about the weather

_____ compliment

_____ make plans to meet later

_1_ greet

_____ end the conversation

_____ introduce

7 ∩ Play track 2 again. Answer each question with a complete sentence.

1. Where does Tom live?

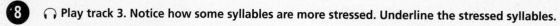
He lives in New York.

2. What is Tom doing in San Diego?

_____

3. How is Sue doing?

_____

4. What company is Tom working at now?

_____

5. Who is Sue working with at West Coast Advertising?

_____

6. In what area is Sue doing her master's degree?

_____

Pronunciation

8 ∩ Play track 3. Notice how some syllables are more stressed. Underline the stressed syllables.

1. <u>How</u> are you <u>doing</u>?

2. Great. What about you?

3. So, how do you like California?

4. It's great. I love the weather here.

5. It was good to see you again.

6. Why don't you give me a call?

9 ∩ Play track 3 again. Listen and repeat.

Why women iron

Vocabulary ⬤

1 Match the pictures to the adjectives in the box.

| aggressive | cooperative | ~~competitive~~ | emotional |
| hardworking | messy | noisy | talkative |

1. competitive
2. _____
3. _____
4. _____

5. _____
6. _____
7. _____
8. _____

2 Ellen and Tim are looking at old photos. Complete their conversation with adjectives from Exercise 1.

Ellen: It's been a long time since I've seen all these pictures from when we were kids. Look! Here you are on your first day of high school. Of course, you weren't a very good student.

Tim: Yes, I was! I was very **(1)** _____hardworking_____. I always did my homework.

Ellen: You worked a lot more at sports than you did at school work.

Tim: That might be true. Here I am playing soccer. I was really good at that.

Ellen: Yes, you were very **(2)** _____ and if you didn't win, you got very upset.

Tim: Upset? What do you mean? I didn't get upset!

Ellen: Oh, come on! You got into fights all the time, especially with me. You were kind of **(3)** _____, you know.

Tim: No, I wasn't. I was always very calm and quiet. You were the one who started the fights. And you were also **(4)** _____. I couldn't sleep or read while you were in the house.

Ellen: Don't be ridiculous. I was just very friendly and **(5)** _____, not shy and quiet like you. And I was very organized, too.

Tim: Hey, are you saying I was **(6)** _____? That's not true . . .

Ellen: Well, what about this picture of your bedroom then? A picture is worth a thousand words!

Grammar

3 Look at the report cards for Alex and Silvia. Write sentences comparing them using the adjectives in parentheses and *more* or *–er*.

STUDENT REPORT

STUDENT NAME: *Alex Jones*

STUDENT #: *18302*

COURSE	NUMBER	TEACHER	1	2	3	4
Language Arts–Reading	0600-12	Hales, A.	A–	B+		
Language Arts–Writing	0601-12	Hales, A.	A	A+		
Social Studies	0605-12	Hales, A.	B+	A–		
Math	0943-12	Hales, A.	B+	B+		
Art	0609-12	Franklin, R.	A–	A–		
Physical Education	0301-12	Smith, M.	A	A		

TEACHER'S NOTES

Alex is helping me in class and he works well with others. In fact, he works all the time – and he talks all the time too! However, sometimes it is not easy to know how Alex feels because he tends to keep his emotions to himself. When he plays games, he really hates to lose. He keeps everything in its place. He is really a wonderful student.

STUDENT REPORT

STUDENT NAME: *Silvia Morales*

STUDENT #: *29076*

COURSE	NUMBER	TEACHER	1	2	3	4
Language Arts–Reading	0600-12	Hales, A.	A–	A		
Language Arts–Writing	0601-12	Hales, A.	B+	B+		
Social Studies	0605-12	Hales, A.	A	A–		
Math	0943-12	Hales, A.	A	B+		
Music	00403-12	Collins, T.	A	A		
Physical Education	0301-12	Smith, M.	A–	B+		

TEACHER'S NOTES

Silvia is a rather quiet student. She doesn't talk much, and she likes to work alone. She never offers to help other students when they are in groups. She likes sports but doesn't feel the need to win all the time. In fact, she likes to take it easy. She could work on being a little neater. She often has her papers and books scattered all over. Also, when Silvia is happy or sad, everyone in class knows it. She never hides her feelings. All in all, she is a very good student.

1. Alex is <u>more cooperative than Silvia.</u> (cooperative)

2. Alex is _____ (competitive)

3. Alex is _____ (hardworking)

4. Silvia is _____ (messy)

5. Alex is _____ (talkative)

6. Silvia is _____ (emotional)

4 Write six more sentences comparing Alex and Silvia. This time use *as . . . as* or *not as . . . as*.

1. <u>Silvia isn't as cooperative as Alex.</u> (cooperative)

2. _____ (competitive)

3. _____ (hardworking)

4. _____ (messy)

5. _____ (talkative)

6. _____ (emotional)

Listening

5 🎧 Play track 4. Listen to the first part of the review of the book *Why Men Don't Iron*. What do the authors say about the differences between boys and girls? Check (✓) the correct column.

	Boys	Girls
1. messier	✓	
2. more competitive		
3. better students		
4. more hardworking		
5. more talkative		
6. noisier		
7. stronger when babies		
8. stronger when older		

6 🎧 Play track 4 again. Listen to the second part of the book review. The authors say a lot of people think men should change. Circle the ways the "new man" should behave, according to some people.

The new man should be . . .

1. more talkative / more cooperative

2. less aggressive / less competitive

3. neater / calmer

4. more emotional / more hardworking

5. better listener / better communicator

Pronunciation

7 🎧 Play track 64. Fill in the blanks in the sentences. Notice the pronunciation of the adjective phrases.

1. Men are ___taller___ ___than___ women.

2. Girls aren't _____ _____ _____ boys.

3. Boys are _____ _____ girls.

4. Women are _____ _____ _____ men.

5. Women are _____ _____ _____ men.

6. Men are _____ _____ women.

7. In school, boys aren't _____ _____ _____ girls.

8. Girls aren't _____ _____ _____ boys at soccer.

8 🎧 Play track 64 again. Listen and repeat.

Living in luxury

Vocabulary

1 Fill in the blanks using the words in the box. Then complete the crossword puzzle.

~~business~~	ballroom	casino	conference	restaurant
fitness	pool	café	arcade	court

Across

1 Computers are available in the <u>business</u> center.

3 The hotel has an indoor _____ so don't forget your swim suit.

5 For light snacks any time of the day, visit the _____.

8 The _____ is open for dinner only and you must make reservations.

9 Get your racket and meet me on the tennis _____.

Down

1 The reception will be held in the _____ on the second floor.

2 The sales meeting is in the _____ room.

4 You can play blackjack, roulette, and other games in the _____.

6 If you want to lift weights or exercise, you can go to the _____ center.

7 The video _____ has a lot of cool new games.

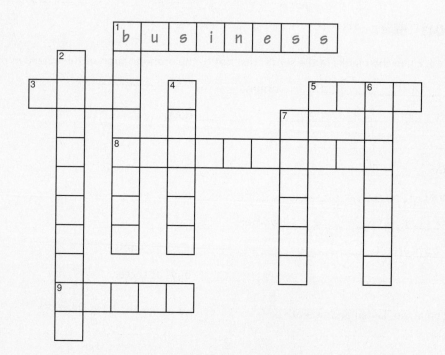

Grammar

2 Look at the brochure for the Downtown Inn. Use the cues to write questions.

DOWNTOWN INN

Brand-new hotel. Free shuttle service from the train station.
45 deluxe guest rooms, 10 with balconies overlooking Park Avenue
Business center with high-speed Internet access
Fitness center and sauna

Many fine restaurants and cafés within five-minute walk of hotel

Basic rates: Single $195; single with balcony $235; double $250;
double with balcony $295; deluxe suite $395

1. number of guest rooms (have)

   How many guest rooms does the hotel have?

2. single room without a balcony (cost)

   _____?

3. restaurant in the hotel (have)

   _____?

4. free shuttle service from the train station (provide)

   _____?

5. swimming pool or fitness center (have)

   _____?

6. Internet access in the room (come with)

   _____?

3 Write answers to the questions in Exercise 2. Use information from the brochure.

1. The hotel has 45 guest rooms.

2. _____

3. _____

4. _____

5. _____

6. _____

Listening 🔊

4 🎧 Play track 6. Listen to the phone conversation between a caller and a reservations clerk at the Four Seasons hotel. The caller took notes, but she made some mistakes. Find and correct five more mistakes.

> 58
> Four Seasons Hotels — ~~26~~ hotels in over 58 countries!
>
> 15,815 rooms
>
> 27,000 employees
>
> Premier Suite — ocean view — $1,400
>
> Deluxe double — without ocean view — $515

5 🎧 Play track 6 again. Complete the reservation information.

FOUR SEASONS

Name: _Lisa and Peter Murphy_

City: _____

Dates: Check in: _____   Check out: _____

Room: _____ (single/double)

Rate: $ _____

Note: Guests celebrating their _____

Pronunciation 🔊

6 🎧 Play track 7. Notice the difference in stress between numbers ending in –*teen* and –*ty*. Underline the stressed syllable in each word.

1. <u>eigh</u>ty   eigh<u>teen</u>   **2.** forty   fourteen   **3.** sixty   sixteen

7 🎧 Play track 7 again. Listen and repeat.

8 🎧 Play track 9. Write the numbers you hear.

1. _13_ minutes   **2.** _____ guest rooms   **3.** _____ guest suites

4. _____ elegant ballrooms   **5.** _____ square feet   **6.** _____ conference rooms

Allergic reactions

Vocabulary

1 Find seven words related to illnesses, across (→) or down (↓). Circle them.

A	S	L	M	O	U	H	L	L	B
E	O	D	A	D	H	E	S	I	A
A	R	R	B	S	S	A	T	E	C
R	E	S	T	E	N	D	O	A	S
A	T	S	I	N	E	A	M	R	O
C	H	V	T	H	R	C	A	M	R
H	R	C	O	L	D	H	C	T	T
E	O	U	A	C	H	E	H	C	E
O	A	L	T	B	A	L	A	M	O
L	T	B	A	C	K	A	C	H	E
E	I	U	B	R	A	S	H	Y	M
T	Y	P	M	U	S	S	E	P	L

2 Complete the sentences with words from Exercise 1.

1. If you have an _____earache_____, you should not go swimming.

2. Listening to loud music for a long time can give you a _____.

3. If you have a _____, you should not carry heavy things.

4. Eating spicy foods can give you a _____.

5. If you have a _____, try not to scratch too much, or it could get worse.

6. When I have a _____, I always take a lot of Vitamin C.

7. You should try not to talk if you have a severe _____.

Grammar

3 Read the advertisement for a counseling service. Circle the correct form of the adjectives.

New City Counseling Service

Is there a lot of stress in your life? Do you often feel unhappy, (1) **frustrated** / frustrating, or (2) **depressed / depressing**? Are you easily (3) **irritated / irritating** by things you didn't mind in the past? Or are you often (4) **tired / tiring** or (5) **bored / boring** and can't find anything (6) **excited / exciting** to do anymore?

Well, you are not alone. It might be (7) **interested / interesting** for you to know that many people suffer from these (8) **annoyed / annoying** symptoms at some point in their lives. The situation seems (9) **frightened / frightening**, but it doesn't have to be that way.

Take a positive step toward improving your life today. Contact us and schedule an appointment with one of our counselors. You'll be (10) **surprised / surprising** how easy it is. Call or email us today!

4 Julia is writing to the counseling service. Find four more errors in the email and correct them.

To: New City Counseling Service
From: Julia

Dear New City Counseling Service:

     tired
I feel so ~~tiring~~ lately. Even getting up in the morning and taking a shower is tiring for me. I'm just

not interesting in anything anymore. I don't have any energy, and the situation is getting really annoyed.

It's frustrated to me, and I'm starting to get depressed. I'm worried that I might lose my job. I just don't

know what to do. I'm too embarrassing to talk to anyone about this problem. Can you help me?

Sincerely,

Julia

Listening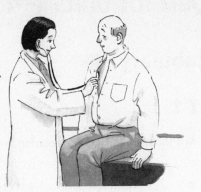

5 🎧 Play track 10. Listen to Doctor Monica talk about allergies. Match each person with the way he or she felt.

1. Sarah _____   a. embarrassed

2. Silvia _____   b. annoyed

3. Fabio _____   c. depressed

6 🎧 Play track 10 again. Match each person with his or her allergies. Make three true statements.

Person	Symptom	Cause
Fabio	headaches	allergic to animals
Silvia	cold	allergic to chocolate
Sarah	a rash	allergic to pollen

Pronunciation

7 🎧 Play track 11. Notice the different pronunciation of the adjectives. Check (✓) the adjectives in which the *-ed* ending is pronounced as an extra syllable.

_____ relaxed   _____ frustrated

_____ bored   _____ surprised

 excited   _____ shocked

_____ tired   _____ frightened

_____ disappointed   _____ interested

_____ depressed   _____ embarrassed

_____ annoyed

8 🎧 Play track 11 again. Listen and repeat.

Self-Quiz for Units 1–4

Vocabulary

UNIT 1

A Put the lines of the conversation in the correct order.

a. _____ Not bad. It's been really busy at work. We opened a new office.

b. _____ Yes. I like sales a lot. Well, I have to get going. Good to see you again.

c. _____ Fine, Alex. How's it going for you?

d. _____ Are you still working in sales?

e. __1__ Hi, Ramon. How are you doing?

f. _____ Yeah, it's good to see you, too. Bye.

UNIT 2

B Complete the sentences with *competitive, cooperative, emotional, hardworking, messy,* or *noisy.* (You won't need all the words.)

1. Tim is very _hardworking_ . He usually gets to work early and often stays late.

2. My brother is so _____! He leaves his clothes and books everywhere.

3. It was difficult to hear the announcements in the _____ train station.

4. My friend isn't very _____. She doesn't say much unless she knows you well.

5. The teacher asked us to be more _____. She encouraged us to help one another.

6. The audience became very _____ when the movie ended. Some people cried quietly.

UNIT 3

C Use the words in the box to complete the description of the hotel. (You won't need all the words.)

ballroom	business center	conference rooms	fitness center	lobby
restaurants	shuttle service	swimming pool	~~video arcade~~	

Our newly renovated hotel has a beautiful
(1) _fitness center_ where guests can exercise.
There is also a large indoor (2) _____,
which guests can use even in bad weather. There
are several (3) _____ on the first floor
for business meetings. The (4) _____
off the main (5) _____ has computers
and high-speed Internet access. Most guest rooms
have Internet access as well. The hotel provides
(6) _____ to and from the airport. For
our hungry guests, there are three gourmet
(7) _____ to choose from.

UNIT 4

D Rewrite the sentences with *have* and the name of the illness.

1. My stomach is upset. _I have a stomachache._

2. I have a sore back. _____

3. My throat hurts. _____

4. I have a pain in my ear. _____

5. My head hurts. _____

6. There are itchy red spots on my arms. _____

24

Grammar

UNIT 1

A Underline the correct form of the verb in the sentences.

1. Mr. Nelson **works** / **is working** too much these days. He **needs** / **is needing** a break.

2. My wife and I **want** / **are wanting** to take an exciting vacation. We **think** / **are thinking** about a trip to Hawaii.

3. Toshi **looks** / **is looking** happy today. He **does** / **is doing** very well both at work and at school.

UNIT 2

B Rewrite the sentences so that they have the same meaning.

1. Daniel is more talkative than Juan. Juan isn't _as talkative as Daniel._

2. Daniel isn't as competitive as Juan. Juan is _____

3. Teresa is messier than Anna. Anna is _____

4. Bob is taller than Steve. Steve isn't _____

5. Keiko is better than Toshi at math. Toshi isn't _____

6. Pedro isn't as emotional as Jon. Jon is _____

UNIT 3

C Complete the conversation with the simple present of the verb in parentheses.

A: **(1)** _Do you have_ (you / have) any rooms available for tonight?

B: We **(2)** _____ (not have) any suites available, but there are deluxe double rooms available.

A: That's fine.

B: **(3)** _____ (you / want) a room with an ocean view? There's a nice room on the second floor, but unfortunately, it **(4)** _____ (not have) a balcony.

A: That's OK. I **(5)** _____ (not need) a balcony. How much **(6)** _____ (the deluxe double / cost) per night?

B: It's $189. That **(7)** _____ (not include) taxes, of course.

UNIT 4

D Circle the correct adjectives to complete the sentences.

1. We were **surprising** / **surprised** to hear that our friend was in the hospital.

2. This cough is really **annoyed** / **annoying**. I can't sleep at night because I start coughing the minute I lie down.

3. The little boy was **frightened** / **frightening** of dogs after a small poodle bit him on the hand.

4. We were **disappointed** / **disappointing** to hear that the trip was canceled.

5. That movie was **bored** / **boring**! I got so **bored** / **boring**, I fell asleep!

6. Doctors are **interested** / **interesting** in learning about treatments for serious illnesses.

5 A typical day

Vocabulary

1 Circle the noun in each group that does not usually go with the verb.

1. deliver — a letter, a message, (a meeting)
2. hire — a person, a ~~movie~~, an assistant
3. make — a call, money, a ~~letter~~, *an appointment, make time*
4. pay — ~~time~~, a bill, money
5. send — a ~~phone~~, a fax, a letter
6. spend — time, money, ~~bills~~
7. take — a picture, a meeting, time
8. take out — an ~~appointment~~, the trash, someone

2 Complete the sentences with verbs from Exercise 1.

1. If you don't _____pay_____ your bills on time, your may have problems later.

2. Many people these days prefer to _____ electronic birthday cards instead of mailing paper cards.

3. Companies often check a person's references before they _____ him or her.

4. It isn't always possible to _____ a cellphone call from the mountains, because reception can be bad.

5. Most Europeans _____ vacations in August.

6. Television and the Internet are among the main reasons families _____ less time together.

7. Arguing about who has to _____ the trash is common in many families around the world.

8. A lot of companies will _____ anything to your home: food, books, and even DVDs.

26

Grammar

3 Read Jim's journal. Use the cues to write questions in the simple present tense about the journal.

> June 20
>
> My older sister Alicia and I have an argument about the bathroom every morning. I like to sleep until about 8:00 A.M., and I get up at 8:15. This means I only have 25 minutes to get ready before I leave the house to catch the 8:40 bus to school.
>
> Alicia always gets up around 7:00 A.M. and then she spends hours in the bathroom. I get really angry. Her classes don't start until 10:00, and she never leaves the house before 9:30, but she's always in the bathroom when I need it. Alicia is never late for class. I'm late every day!
>
> Alicia always tells me to get up earlier. I tell her to use the bathroom after I'm done. Then Mom tells us both to be quiet. This isn't a good way to start the day.

1. who / Jim / argue with

Who does Jim argue with?

2. who / be / never late for class

_____

3. who / the 8:40 bus / catch

_____

4. who / get up / at 7 A.M.

_____

5. who / Jim / get / angry with

_____

6. who / spend / hours in the bathroom

_____

7. who / tell / Alicia and Jim to be quiet

_____

Listening

4 🎧 **Play track 12. Listen to the interview with Ron. Answer the questions.**

1. Why is a singing telegram better than a greeting card?

   It's more memorable and original.

2. What are two occasions that Ron composes songs for?

3. What is "Say It with a Song?"

4. Who takes pictures of Ron delivering the telegram?

5. Who forgets a singing telegram?

5 🎧 **Play track 12 again. Write the questions the interviewer asks Ron.**

I: **(1)** ___*Is it expensive to send someone a singing telegram*___ ?

R: Not really. Each singing telegram costs about $50.

I: **(2)** _____ ?

R: Actually, I work for an agency called "Say it with a Song."

I: So let's say I want to send a singing telegram to my wife. **(3)** _____ ?

R: Just make a phone call. Call the agency and tell them you want to hire me, Ron Bates, to deliver a singing telegram. (…) Then just wait for the special day when I show up at your wife's workplace and deliver your singing telegram.

I: **(4)** _____ ? Do I pay you or the agency?

R: The agency. Then the agency pays me.

I: I guess you don't work alone. **(5)** _____ ?

R: My wife, Mary. She buys some flowers. Then she comes with me and takes a picture as I give the person flowers and sing the song.

I: **(6)** _____ ?

R: No, not really. I love singing, and I like to make people happy. And, you know, no one forgets a singing telegram.

Pronunciation

6 🎧 **Play track 13. Listen. Notice how the voice goes up on some words. These are the focus words. Circle the focus word in each sentence.**

Who gets up first in your house?   Usually I do.

7 🎧 **Play track 65. Listen. Fill in the blanks with the focus words.**

1. And who do you have ___*breakfast*___ with?

2. Who uses the _____ the most in your house?

3. Who do you _____ the most?

4. Who do you _____ more time with, your _____ or your _____ ?

It's absolutely true!

Vocabulary

1 Fill in the blanks with words from the box.

awful	bad	~~big~~	boiling	cold	crowded	~~enormous~~
exhausted	freezing	good	fantastic	hot	packed	tired

1. He wasn't just _____big_____, he was _enormous_ !

2. She ran a double marathon—she wasn't _____, she was _____.

3. Her haircut isn't just _____, it's _____ !

4. I'm not _____, I'm _____ !

5. They're not _____ dancers, they're _____ !

6. The subway is usually _____, but at eight in the morning it's _____.

7. I asked for a _____ chocolate, but this is _____ !

2 Complete the sentences with words *really*, *absolutely*, or *very*. Some sentences will have more than one correct answer.

1. The movie was _____really_____ awful— don't bother going to see it.

2. I really need to go to bed. I'm _____ exhausted.

3. There were no seats on the bus. It was _____ crowded.

4. He has _____ big feet — it's difficult for him to find shoes that fit.

5. Their new house has five bedrooms and three bathrooms. It is _____ enormous.

6. There were over 100,000 people in the stadium — it was _____ packed!

7. I just love musicals, and I thought *The Lion King* was _____ fantastic.

Grammar

3 Read the text and complete each sentence with the correct form of the verbs in parentheses. Use the simple past or the past continuous. Some blanks can have two correct answers.

Lost!

It was late afternoon in Antarctica and time for Keizo Funatsu to feed the dogs. Keizo and five other men **(1)** were traveling **(travel)** across Antarctica by dog sled and had stopped to set up camp. It **(2)** _____ **(snow)** lightly when Keizo **(3)** _____ **(go)** outside. Suddenly, it **(4)** _____ **(begin)** to snow harder and the wind **(5)** _____ **(become)** much stronger. In a few minutes, the weather changed from bad to absolutely awful and Keizo couldn't find his tent in the snow.

He **(6)** _____ **(carry)** only one tool. He used it to dig a hole in the snow for shelter. While he **(7)** _____ **(dig)**, he **(8)** _____ **(feel)** warm. But when he **(9)** _____ **(stop)**, he **(10)** _____ **(realize)** how cold he was.

Keizo's friends **(11)** _____ **(shout)** and looking for him. But the wind **(12)** _____ **(blow)** so hard, that they **(13)** _____ **(not hear)** him. It **(14)** _____ **(begin)** to get dark. During the night, Keizo no longer just felt cold – he was freezing!

At 5:00 A.M., it started to get light. But Keizo still could not see anything – just white all around him. Then Keizo **(15)** _____ **(hear)** a voice. At first, he **(16)** _____ **(think)** it was just the sound of the wind, but the voice **(17)** _____ **(come)** closer. When his friends **(18)** _____ **(find)** him, Keizo **(19)** _____ **(shout)** "I'm alive! I'm alive!" They helped him back to his tent. He was only a short distance away, but during the storm it was impossible to see. Keizo was lost in a place with some of the worst weather in the world!

4 Answer the questions about the article in Exercise 3.

1. Where were Keizo and the other five men traveling?

They were traveling in Antarctica.

2. What was the weather like when they stopped to set up their camp?

_____

3. How many tools was Keizo carrying?

_____

4. What were Keizo's friends doing while he was lost?

_____

5. What did Keizo do when his friends found him?

_____

Listening

5 ⌒ **Play track 16. Listen to the friends' conversation. Circle the phrase that best describes Sara's vacation.**

absolutely fantastic   very crowded   really awful

6 ⌒ **Play track 16 again. Write *T* (true) or *F* (false) next to each sentence. If the sentence is false, correct it.**

1. Sara went to São Paolo, Brazil, on her vacation.   F

Sara went to Rio de Janeiro, Brazil, on her vacation.

2. The tourists were all on the beach.

_____

3. Brazil is absolutely freezing in February.

_____

4. The Sambadrome is an enormous store.

_____

5. It rained all during Carnaval.

_____

6. The Carnaval parade could not start on time.

_____

7. Sara was absolutely exhausted after Carnaval.

_____

Pronunciation

7 ⌒ **Play track 66. Listen. Notice the number of syllables and the stress. Write the number of syllables you hear in each word.**

fantastic _3_   packed _____   interesting _____   fascinating _____   freezing _____

enormous _____   crowded _____   boiling _____   exhausted _____   tired _____

8 ⌒ **Play track 66 again. Underline the stressed syllable in each word in Exercise 7.**

fantastic   packed   interesting   fascinating   freezing

enormous   crowded   boiling   exhausted   tired

9 ⌒ **Play track 66 again. Listen and repeat.**

UNIT 7

Eating out

Vocabulary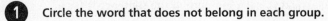

1 Circle the word that does not belong in each group.

1. bland	salty	(formal)	sour
2. casual	rude	elegant	formal
3. rude	polite	indifferent	romantic
4. low-fat	healthful	spicy	nutritious
5. courteous	hot	sweet	greasy

2 Complete the conversation with adjectives from Exercise 1.

A: I'm taking Lisa out for dinner tomorrow. Where should we go?

B: I know you like fancy restaurants. I'd go to The Greenhouse. It's very
(1) _____elegant_____ .

A: What about Danielle's? It's a perfect restaurant for a first date. It's a very
(2) _____ place with white tablecloths and red roses on the tables.

B: Well, Danielle's might not be the best place. Lisa is into (3) _____ food
and Danielle's sauces are a bit rich.

A: What about the new vegetarian restaurant on Park Avenue? I heard they serve very
(4) _____ food, with no additives or heavy sauces.

B: It's not bad, but it's a bit (5) _____ for a first date. You know, no
tablecloths, no reservations . . . I'd go for something more formal, like Emilio's.

A: You're probably right, but I'm not crazy about Emilio's. The service is horrible. Last
time I went, I told the waiter that my soup was cold, and what did he do? Nothing!
It's not that they're (6) _____ or anything, but they're totally indifferent.

B: I'll tell you what. Go to Tavern on the Square. They serve very healthful food, not
salty or spicy, but not (7) _____ either. The waiters are very
(8) _____ and polite. You'll love it.

A: That sounds like an excellent choice. Thanks.

Grammar

3 Complete the sentences with *too* or *enough* and the correct set of words from the box.

strong / me / drink	do / exercise	~~not cold / be safe to drink~~	spicy / children
greasy / me	quiet / business lunch	not formal / business dinner	

1. The milk _wasn't cold enough to be safe to drink._

2. The chicken with hot pepper was _____.

3. Their donuts are _____.

4. If you _____, you can eat anything you want.

5. None of the restaurants near the university is _____.

6. The coffee was much _____.

7. The Corner Café is _____.

4 Susie wrote to her friend about a restaurant experience. Correct six more errors in her email.

To: Ellen
From: Susie

Hi Ellen:

We went to City Escapes tonight and didn't have a very good time. First, we had to wait for a table because the place is small. There ~~is enough room~~ *isn't enough room* between the tables, so you don't have any privacy when you speak. Then came the food. The fish was not enough fresh, it didn't have salt enough, and it was overcooked. To make things worse, the tea wasn't enough hot. I know I shouldn't complain about prices because I didn't pay, but everything was too much expensive. The service wasn't very good either. The restaurant doesn't have waiters enough, and they weren't enough attentive. The manager must not be enough strict with them. When we complained, the manager did give us free desserts, but they were too sweet!

See you soon,

Susie

Listening

5 Play track 19. Listen to the restaurant review. Check (✓) the menu items the reviewer mentions.

calamari ✓

cheesecake _____

chicken _____

chocolate ice cream _____

double chocolate cake _____

fish _____

fruit salad _____

Mexican appetizers _____

stuffed mushrooms _____

peach tart _____

salad _____

steak _____

6 Play track 19 again. Complete the statements with the reviewer's opinion.

1. The Palm is _____ *quiet enough* _____ for a business meeting.

2. The specials make the menu _____.

3. The appetizer menu is _____.

4. The Mexican appetizers were a little _____ for me.

5. There is _____ variety on the dessert menu.

Pronunciation

7 Play tracks 17 and 18. Notice the short, unclear sound /ə/ vowels in each word. Circle them.

casual   nutritious   healthful   indifferent

polite   formal   elegant   courteous

8 Play tracks 17 and 18 again. Listen and repeat.

It's a deal!

Vocabulary

1 Circle the word that does not follow the verb.

1. make   an agreement, a decision, (a job)

2. react to   a situation, the bills, problems

3. take care of   financial obligations, the housework, a decision

4. do   an agreement, the dishes, the housework

5. have   arguments, a prenuptial agreement, danger

6. lose   a job, his temper, an agreement

7. sign   a contract, a decision, a prenuptial agreement

8. exchange   problems, wedding rings, gifts

2 Complete the letter to the self-help columnist using verb-noun combinations from Exercise 1. Use the appropriate form of the verb.

Dear Andrea:

I just got married, and from the moment we **(1)** <u>exchanged wedding rings</u> at our wedding ceremony, my husband Mike and I have been having terrible arguments about money. You see, I have a good job and make a lot of money, but Mike is an actor and it's hard for him to make money, so I pay all the bills. I don't mind if I have to **(2)** _____, especially when he's not working. However, I expected him to stay home and **(3)** _____ while I'm at the office. But when I suggest that he wash the dishes or take out the trash, he gets angry and often **(4)** _____. Before we got married, some friends told me that we should **(5)** _____ so that things would be clear from the start. I didn't think it was necessary because I thought marriage wasn't just an agreement that requires the bride and groom to **(6)** _____. Well, I was wrong. Now our marriage is in serious danger, and I just don't know what to do.

Signed,
Money-Troubled Marriage

Grammar

3 Complete the sentences with the correct form of *(don't) have to* or *can't*.

1. You / buy tickets online. They're available at the box office only.

   <u>You can't buy the tickets online.</u>

2. I / get up at 6 A.M. every day. It takes me two hours to get to work.

   _____

3. You / buy the tickets in advance. It's OK to buy them at the door the day of the concert.

   _____

4. What time / you get up in the morning?

   _____

5. If the bride signs a prenuptial agreement, the groom / sign it, too. Otherwise, it's not valid.

   _____

6. In many countries, you / get married before you're eighteen.

   _____

7. Not every contract / be written by a lawyer, but it's always good advice to contact one for any legal matter.

   _____

4 Use the verbs in the box to write sentences explaining what each sign says you *must do* or *cannot (can't) do*.

turn   stop   bicycle   walk   park   enter   fish   ~~talk~~   buckle

1. <u>You can't talk.</u>   2. _____   3. _____   4. _____

5. _____   6. _____   7. _____   8. _____

Listening

5 Play track 20. Listen to the information about prenuptial agreements. Who has to do what in the prenuptial agreement mentioned? Place a check (✓) in the correct columns.

	Susan	Bruce
Do the housework		✓
Cook dinner		
Pay the bills		

6 Play track 20 again. Write *T* (true) or *F* (false) after each sentence. If the sentence is false, correct it.

1. Prenuptial agreements are only for very rich people. F

    Prenuptials are not only for very rich people.

2. Bruce makes a lot more money than Susan.

3. Bruce is a math teacher, and Susan is a doctor.

4. If they get divorced, Bruce can ask Susan for money.

5. At first, Bruce was angry about the prenuptial agreement.

6. Bruce and Susan have a sort of "marriage insurance."

Pronunciation

7 Play track 67. Notice the weak pronunciation of *have to* and *has to*. Complete the sentence with the phrase you hear.

1. _____I have to_____ see a doctor.

2. _____ come to the party.

3. _____ do the housework.

4. _____ do the shopping?

5. _____ give her a lot of money.

6. _____ sign an agreement?

8 Play track 67 again. Listen and repeat.

Self-Quiz for Units 5–8

Vocabulary

UNIT 5

A   Write the verb that usually goes with the nouns.

make	pay	~~send~~	spend	take	take out

1. ___send___ an email message, a letter

2. _____ my bills, the check

3. _____ the trash, the dog

4. _____ a phone call, an appointment

5. _____ a vacation, a break

6. _____ time, money

UNIT 6

B   Match the sentences on the left with the responses on the right.

1. Was the movie good? __c__

2. Are you tired from your trip? _____

3. Was it cold in the mountains? _____

4. I heard the new hotel is big. _____

5. Was the party very crowded? _____

6. Wasn't it hot last night? _____

   a. Yes, it was absolutely boiling!

   b. It was really packed!

   c. Yes, it was fantastic!

   d. We're all really exhausted!

   e. It's absolutely enormous!

   f. It was freezing!

UNIT 7

C   Replace the underlined words with their opposites. Use *bland, casual, elegant, healthful, indifferent, polite, romantic,* or *sour.* (You won't need all the words.)

                                          bland

1. I didn't like that restaurant. The food was much too ~~spicy~~.

2. That restaurant is known for its <u>rude</u> service.

3. Mrs. Thomas and her friends prefer to go to <u>formal</u> restaurants.

4. This soup is too <u>sweet</u>. I can't eat it.

5. I don't think that restaurant is <u>casual</u> enough for the office party.

6. The reviewer said that he enjoyed this restaurant's <u>rich</u> food.

UNIT 8

D   Match the categories on the left with the examples on the right.

1. types of contracts __b__

2. types of housework _____

3. financial obligations _____

4. things we lose _____

5. things we exchange _____

6. things we sign _____

   a. letters, contracts

   b. leases, prenuptial agreements

   c. wedding rings, email messages

   d. credit-card bills, rent

   e. our tempers, weight

   f. cooking, ironing

Grammar

UNIT 5

A   Read the sentences. Write questions with *who* based on the underlined words or phrases. Use a separate piece of paper.

1. <u>Antonio</u> usually cooks dinner.   *Who usually cooks dinner?*

2. Raj almost always eats dinner <u>with his family</u>.

3. <u>Sara</u> gets up at 6:00 A.M.

4. Sylvia spends her free time <u>with her friends</u>.

5. <u>Juan</u> is often late to class.

6. Dan irritates <u>his boss</u> when he comes to work late.

UNIT 6

B   Complete the sentences with the correct form of the verb in parentheses. Use the simple past or past continuous.

1. Lee ___was waiting___ (wait) for his bus when he _____ (see) a car accident.

2. Tara _____ (walk) down the beach when it _____ (start) raining.

3. As I _____ (open) the door, I _____ (hear) the phone ringing.

4. It _____ (snow) when our plane _____ (arrive) in Boston.

5. After Dan _____ (eat) breakfast, he _____ (get) ready for work.

UNIT 7

C   Put the words in the correct order to write sentences. Add capital letters and punctuation where needed. Use a separate piece of paper.

1. too / the / demanding / was / customer   *The customer was too demanding.*

2. hot / for / coffee / wasn't / enough / the / me

3. lunch-time / Italian / too / restaurant / for / that / noisy / a / meeting / is

4. on / aren't / low-fat / this / enough / there / foods / menu

5. tomato / the / was / us / soup / salty / too / for

6. him / for / too / dessert / was / chocolate / the / sweet

UNIT 8

D   Complete the conversation with the correct form of *must, have to, don't have to,* or *can't.* More than one answer is possible in some cases.

Tina: We **(1)** ___have to___ buy our airline tickets for our trip.

Rob: It's late and we **(2)** _____ call the travel agent. Let's go online.

Tina: OK. We **(3)** _____ buy the tickets tonight, but we can at least check prices.

Rob: Actually, now that I think about it, we **(4)** _____ buy the tickets until I talk to my boss. I **(5)** _____ find out when I can be away from the office.

Tina: Well, you **(6)** _____ do that tomorrow. We **(7)** _____ wait any longer.

UNIT 9

The river

Vocabulary

1   Circle the phrasal verb with the same or similar meaning to the underlined word or phrase.

1. My car <u>stopped working</u> again and now I have to cancel our trip.

     broke up   broke off   (broke down)   broke away

2. Tomorrow Ted and I are going camping. We're going to <u>start our trip</u> at 6:00 in the morning. I hope I can wake up that early!

     head off   head out   head in   head for

3. My wife and I were in Chicago last weekend. Our friend Maya <u>let us stay at her apartment</u>.

     put us up   put us away   put us down   put us off

4. We're visiting some friends in Seoul next weekend. They're going to <u>give us a tour of the city</u>.

     show us up   show us in   show us around   show us off

5. I went to Mexico for a business trip last month. I was in Mexico City for only two days. Then I <u>continued</u> to Veracruz and finally to Puebla.

     went for   went on   went around   went out

6. Our tour of Hollywood <u>began</u> on Sunset Boulevard.

     started off   started in   started on   started up

7. As soon as I <u>left</u> the train, I called my office.

     got away   got on   got ahead   got off

2   Complete the paragraph with the phrasal verbs in Exercise 1.

Our trip to Egypt was really interesting—in many ways! We arrived at our hotel in Cairo with no problem. But to visit the pyramids, we had to **(1)** _____head out_____ at 5 A.M. to avoid the crowds. On the way there, our bus

(2) _____. We all **(3)** _____ the bus and walked the rest of the way. By the time we reached the pyramids, the place was full of tourists.

A guide offered to **(4)** _____, so we hired him. He was very kind and offered to **(5)** _____ at his home for the evening. But we told him we already had a nice hotel in Cairo, and said "No, thank you." Then we

(6) _____ to visit the Khan el Khalili bazaar.

Grammar

Complete the sentences with the appropriate form of the verbs in parentheses. Use the simple present or present continuous for future.

Joe: What <u>are you doing</u> tonight?
        <small>1. (you / do)</small>

Pam: I _____ to the movies with Ken.
        <small>2. (go)</small>

Joe: Sounds like fun. What movie _____?
        <small>3. (you / see)</small>

Pam: The new Jennifer Lopez film. Do you want to come? It _____ at 7:45.
        <small>4. (start)</small>

Joe: Oh, no, thanks, I can't. I _____ late.
        <small>5. (work)</small>

Pam: Again? That's awful!

Joe: I know, but I _____ for São Paulo on Monday and I have a lot to do.
        <small>6. (leave)</small>

Pam: _____ into the office on Monday?
        <small>7. (you / come)</small>

Joe: Yes. My flight _____ until 10:20 P.M.
        <small>8. (not leave)</small>

Pam: So late? What time _____ in São Paulo?
        <small>9. (you / land)</small>

Joe: At 9:46 the next morning. It takes 9½ hours.

Pam: I hope you can sleep on the plane! _____ you at the airport?
        <small>10. (someone / meet)</small>

Joe: Yes. Marcela and Jairo.

Find and correct nine more errors in the email.

To: Jong-Min
From: Ho-Young

Hi, Jong-Min.

Guess what! I ~~go~~ 'm going to Seattle with my friends, Mon and Frank, on Saturday. We take a bus. It's a long trip—about six hours. The bus is leaving at 11:00 and we're arriving in Seattle at 5:00.

In Seattle, we stay at a hotel near the Space Needle. The first morning, we take a walking tour of different neighborhoods. In the afternoon, we're going to the Pike Place Market. After that, we're having coffee at the first Starbuck's! For dinner, we eat at a great sushi bar. Then we meet friends of Mon's in the Capitol Hill district. There are a lot of music clubs there.

The next day, we visit the Space Needle, the Pacific Science Center, and Experience Music Project. We have dinner that night at a restaurant that Mon's friends recommended. If we're not too tired, we're going out to a dance club after dinner.

We get back home late on Tuesday. I'll call you on Wednesday, OK?

Ho-Young

Listening

5 Play track 22. Listen to the tourist and the travel agent. Look at the tourist's notes. Number the tour activities in the correct order.

> _____ go to the theater
>
> _____ meet Raul for dinner
>
> _1_ head out from Kingston
>
> _____ see Richmond Park and Kew Gardens
>
> _____ go past the Houses of Parliament, Tate Modern, and Globe Theatre
>
> _____ tour Hampton Court

6 Play track 22 again. The tourist asks the travel agent several questions. Check (✓) the ones you hear.

1. a. What time does the boat actually head out from Kingston? __✔__

  b. What time does the boat actually depart from Kingston? _____

2. a. How long do we stay at Hampton Court? _____

  b. How long are we planning to stay at Hampton Court? _____

3. a. How about the evening? _____

  b. What about the evening? _____

4. a. What about the next day? _____

  b. What about Tuesday? _____

Pronunciation

7 Play track 23. Draw linking lines where a consonant or vowel at the end of a word is linked to a vowel at the beginning of the next word.

1. When does the boat head out?

2. We get off at Hampton Court.

3. A guide will show us around.

4. Then we go on to the park.

5. A friend is putting me up.

8 Play track 23 again. Listen and repeat.

On the other hand

Vocabulary

1 Circle the word or expression that does not belong in each group.

1. hard	complicated	challenging	(no trouble)
2. simple	tough	manageable	straightforward
3. impossible	complicated	challenging	a piece of cake
4. a piece of cake	simple	no trouble	complicated
5. challenging	impossible	manageable	tough

2 Underline the correct word to complete each sentence.

1. Some yoga poses are quite simple, but others are almost **impossible / challenging**.

2. The first time you use a computer it seems **simple / complicated**.

3. My father has worked on cars all his life, so changing a tire is **tough / a piece of cake** for him.

4. I've lived in Korea for 20 years, so speaking Korean is **no trouble / hard** for me now.

5. The job seems difficult now, but over time it will get more and more **impossible / manageable**.

6. I love to cook, so cooking for eight people was really **no trouble / complicated**.

7. If you use the Internet often, doing research can be quite **simple / complicated**.

8. It's **tough / no trouble** to become an Olympic athlete even if you begin training at a very young age.

10

Grammar

3 Rewrite the sentences. Use the correct form of the verbs in parentheses.

1. She's able to write with either hand.

_She can write with either hand._____ **(can)**

2. My dad can speak five languages.

_____ **(be able to)**

3. We haven't been able to see the baby yet.

_____ **(manage)**

4. The weather was bad, so I wasn't able to take any photos.

_____ **(could)**

5. It was difficult, but I managed to do it.

_____ **(be able to)**

6. I could swim when I was four.

_____ **(be able to)**

4 Complete the advertisement with the correct form of *can*, *could*, or *be able to*, plus the verbs in parentheses.

HOME WORKOUT –
For Busy People Just Like **YOU!**

(1) _____Are_____ you __able to find__
(find) time to exercise during your busy day?

(2)_____ you _____
(fit) in the clothes you wore 10 years ago?

Home Workout has helped others, and it

(3)_____ **(help)** you, too. Here's what

satisfied users of Home Workout have to say.

"Before I got Home Workout, I **(4)**_____
(climb) the stairs to my third-floor apartment without

stopping to catch my breath. I also **(5)**_____ *(fit) into any of my old clothes.*
Now I feel and look great!"

— Maria Gonzales, student

"I **(6)**_____ *(join) a health club because it was too expensive. But with Home Workout,*
I **(7)**_____ *(exercise) anytime."*

— Laurence Zhang, sales assistant

Listening

5   🎧 **Play track 24. Listen to the conversation. Number the activities in the order you hear them.**

A. ____   B. ____   C. _1_   D. ____

6   🎧 **Play track 24 again. Correct the italicized word in each statement.**

easy
1. Throwing the ball was ~~challenging~~ for Mike.

2. Writing was *simple* for Juliana.

3. Mike thinks that using the scissors was *challenging*.

4. Drawing was *hard* for Mike.

5. Drawing was a *piece of cake* for Juliana.

Pronunciation

7   🎧 **Play tracks 25 and 26. Notice the difference in pronunciation of *can/can't* and *could/couldn't*. Circle the word you hear.**

1. She **(can)** / **can't** throw a ball with either hand.

2. I **can** / **can't** draw with my left hand.

3. He **could** / **couldn't** play chess when he was four.

4. I **could** / **couldn't** cook until I got married.

5. They **can** / **can't** dance very well.

6. She **could** / **couldn't** ride a bike.

7. He **can** / **can't** play the guitar.

8. My grandmother **could** / **couldn't** speak English.

9. I **can** / **can't** read without glasses.

10. He **can** / **can't** write with his left hand.

8   🎧 **Play tracks 25 and 26 again. Listen and repeat.**

Trading spaces

Vocabulary

1 Write the words that match each picture. What word does number 10 down make?

1.

10.

S O F A

2.

_ _ _ _ _ _ _ _

3.

_ _ _ _ _ _ _ _ _

4.

_ _ _ _ _ _ _

5.

_ _ _ _ _ _ _ _ _ _

6.

_ _ _ _ _ _ _ _

7.

_ _ _

8.

_ _ _ _ _ _ _ _ _ _ _ _

9.

_ _ _ _ _ _ _ _ _

2 Complete the sentences with words from Exercise 1. Use the plural when necessary.

1. Putting ___rugs___ on the floor can make a cold room feel warmer.

2. Many small _____ or photos on the wall give a touch of personality to a living room.

3. For a less formal look, use blinds instead of drapes for your _____ .

4. A _____ that opens into a bed is great for a small apartment.

5. _____ help keep a house organized, especially if you're a student.

6. In a small apartment, you can use the _____ for eating, working, playing cards—even to iron!

7. An _____ is the ideal place to sit and relax in the evening.

8. For romantic winter evenings, sit by the _____ .

9. An inexpensive way to add color to your living room is to put several _____ on your sofa.

Grammar

3 Read the magazine article. Complete the sentences using the present perfect of the verbs.

Want to shift your fortunes?
Then shift your furniture!

Today many office workers and executives think that the secret to achieving success in business is quite simple – redecorate. But instead of just "redecorating," use "feng shui." This Eastern art of placing particular objects in particular places is said to create a positive business environment. Here are some of the ways this is done:

- An aquarium will attract profits to your door. Stock the fish tank with eight fish, because "eight" means money in the near future.
- When seated behind your desk, make sure you see the door. If your back is toward the door, you may be the victim of dangerous office politics.
- A crystal over the telephone attracts clients, business partners, and even friends. Any glittery glass object could also help.
- Bright light (fire energy) and a tall plant (tree energy) in the southern part of your building will improve sales. The color purple will further enhance this powerful effect.

| buy | hang | ~~install~~ | move | put | stock |

1. Harold wants to make more money, so he ___has installed___ a large aquarium and _____ it with eight goldfish.

2. Elaine and Julie _____ their desks so that they are facing the doorway because they are feeling uncomfortable about office politics.

3. David _____ a small crystal over his telephone because he wants more clients.

4. Jenny _____ a tall plant and she _____ it near the window in her office that faces south. All this because she needs to improve her sales figures!

4 Use the words in parentheses and the present perfect form of the verb.

Interviewer: Welcome to Focus on the Future. Today we're talking to Melinda Chang about feng shui. _How many feng shui consultations have you done?_
1. (How many / feng shui consultations / do?)

Melinda: Oh, I don't know. _____
2. (I / do / so many that I can't remember.)

Interviewer: I see that _____ Why did you do that?
3. (you / bring / four crystals into the studio today.)

Melinda: The crystals clear the room of negative energy, so that we can have a good interview. _____
4. (It / work / very well for me on other interviews.)

Interviewer: I see. _____.
5. (What / scientists / say / about the power of crystals?)

Melinda: _____, but you have
6. (The scientific community / not give / an opinion)
nothing to lose by trying, right?

Interviewer: Right!

Listening

5 Play track 28. Listen to Carla and Pedro talk about the changes in their apartment. Write (+) if the person likes the change, (–) if he or she doesn't, and (?) if you don't know.

Room change	Pedro's reaction	Carla's reaction
Floor	+	
Walls		
Drapes		
Sofa		
Bookcase		

6 Play track 28 again. What have the Nelsons done? Complete the sentences.

1. ___They've redecorated___ the living room.

2. _____ the wood floor.

3. _____ new drapes.

4. _____ the sofa under the window.

5. _____ new covers for the armchairs.

6. _____ the bookcase.

7. _____ the television in the home entertainment center.

Pronunciation

7 Play track 68. Notice the difference in the pronunciation of the letter *a* in each set of words.

Short /a/ sound: armchair lamp

Long /a/ sound: table drapes

8 Play track 69. Listen. Put curved lines above the short /a/ sounds, straight lines above the long /a/ sounds, and no marks over the other sounds.

basket cabinet carpet fireplace

plants bookcase rack

9 Play track 69 again. Listen and repeat.

A soccer fan's website

Vocabulary

1 Complete the sentences with a preposition where necessary.

1. Did you buy the tickets ____on____ Tuesday?

2. The soccer game is _____ Sunday the 13th.

3. Please call me _____ the 10th _____ 9 A.M.

4. Let's have coffee together _____ tomorrow _____ 9:00 A.M.

5. James will be here _____ next week.

6. I usually call my parents _____ the evening.

7. We met _____ eight _____ this morning.

2 Find and correct seven more mistakes in the email.

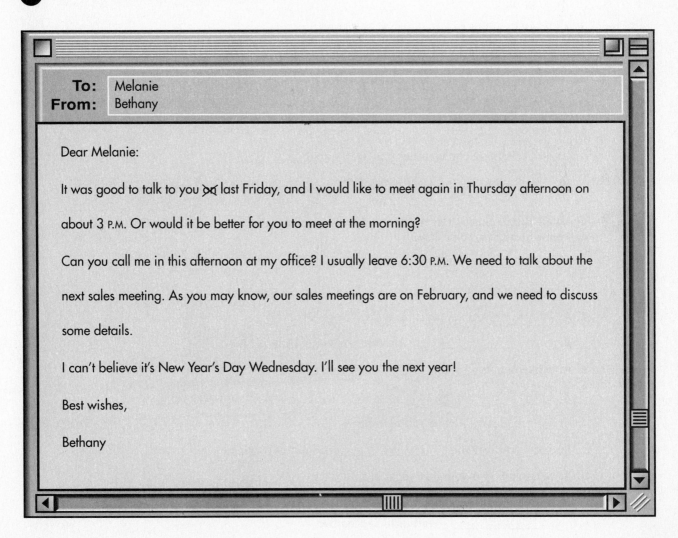

To: Melanie
From: Bethany

Dear Melanie:

It was good to talk to you ~~on~~ last Friday, and I would like to meet again in Thursday afternoon on about 3 P.M. Or would it be better for you to meet at the morning?

Can you call me in this afternoon at my office? I usually leave 6:30 P.M. We need to talk about the next sales meeting. As you may know, our sales meetings are on February, and we need to discuss some details.

I can't believe it's New Year's Day Wednesday. I'll see you the next year!

Best wishes,

Bethany

12 Grammar

3 Complete the conversations with the appropriate modal (*may*, *might*, or *could*) in the affirmative or the negative. More than one answer is possible in some cases.

1. **A:** What's Tiffany going to do with that dollar you gave her?

   B: I'm not sure. She _____ might _____ buy an ice cream cone or she _____ buy a chocolate bar.

2. **A:** Do you know who that woman is?

   B: No, but she _____ be Laura's sister. Why don't you go talk to her?

   A: Oh, I _____ do that. I'm much too shy.

3. **A:** I'm going out tonight with some friends. Would you like to come?

   B: I'd love to, but I _____ be home until very late today.

   A: Maybe you _____ meet us somewhere after work.

   B: OK. I'll call you on your cell phone. I _____ have to work that late, after all.

4. **A:** Are you going to take a taxi to the airport?

   B: No, I'm taking the train. I have to leave at five and there _____ be a lot of traffic.

   A: You're right. It _____ take you forever to get there.

5. **A:** We're having a picnic on Sunday. Would you like to come?

   B: Are you sure? The weather has been so bad, it _____ rain all day!

   A: I don't think so. The weather report mentioned some showers, but nothing serious.

4 Complete the sentences. Use the appropriate form of *may*, *might*, or *could*. More than one answer is possible in some cases.

1. **A:** It's sunny today. Why do you have an umbrella?

   B: The weather report said it _____ might _____ rain later.

2. **A:** Why don't you ask Matt for a ride to the airport?

   B: No, I _____ do that. He's very busy.

3. **A:** Are you going to take English classes next semester?

   B: I have to travel a lot, so I _____, but I'm not sure yet.

4. **A:** Where's Jessica? Have you seen her?

   B: Look upstairs. She _____ be in her room.

5. **A:** When are you going on vacation?

   B: We're not sure yet. We _____ go in August, or we _____ wait until September.

Grammar

3 Complete the conversations with *since* or *for*.

1. A: How long has your wife been away?

   B: Just ___*since*___ Thursday. She'll be back next weekend.

2. A: How long have you worked here at Creative Essence?

   B: _____ almost ten years.

3. A: Have you been a member of this health club for a long time?

   B: No, only _____ September.

4. A: How long have you known Roberto?

   B: _____ I was a little kid. How about you?

   A: I've only known him _____ six months.

5. A: Are you still watching TV?

   B: Yes, Dad. What's the problem? I've only had it on _____ an hour.

   A: That's not true. You've had it on _____ you came home three hours ago.

6. A: I didn't know you had a new car. How long have you had it?

   B: _____ about a month. My parents helped me buy it.

4 Combine the sentences using the present perfect of the verbs in parentheses and *for* or *since*.

1. Peter moved to New York in 1998. He still lives there. **(live)**

   Peter has lived in New York since 1998.

2. Noriko is in the U.S. She arrived two months ago. **(be)**

   _____

3. Susana has a black leather jacket. She bought it four years ago. **(have)**

   _____

4. Victor loves music. He started taking classes when he was five. **(study)**

   _____

5. Patricia met Tim in 2001. They just got engaged. **(know)**

   _____

6. Lucy lives in a new apartment. She moved in last week. **(have)**

   _____

7. I'm a teacher. I became a teacher in 1995. **(be)**

   _____

8. Lorna and Sam are married. They got married a few months ago. **(be)**

   _____

Listening 🔊

5 🎧 Play track 31. Listen to the immigration officer interview Kate Bolton. Number the topics they talk about in the correct order.

_____ **a.** Kate Bolton's job

_____ **b.** things Kate and her husband like to do together

__1__ **c.** how long Kate has been in the U.S.

_____ **d.** where the bathroom is

_____ **e.** how long she has known Rod

_____ **f.** how long they have been married

6 🎧 Play track 31 again. Answer the questions.

1. How long has Kate been in the U.S.?

Kate has been in the U.S. for eight months.

2. How long has she been in New York?

3. Where was Kate staying before she came to New York?

4. How long has Kate known Rod?

5. How long has she been in love with him?

Pronunciation 🔊

7 🎧 Play track 70. Notice the weak pronunciation of _have_ and _has_. Check (✓) the sentence you hear.

1. _____ I told this story to many people already.

✓ I've told this story to many people already.

2. _____ She's visited me several times.

_____ She visited me several times.

3. _____ They lived together in this apartment.

_____ They've lived together in this apartment.

4. _____ I've watched her teach dancing.

_____ I watched her teach dancing.

5. _____ He played football.

_____ He's played football.

8 🎧 Play track 70 again. Listen and repeat.

What's that noise?

Vocabulary

1 What noise do you think the people in the pictures are making? Choose from the words in the box.

| clap | ~~scream~~ | laugh | shout | cheer | yawn | whistle | cry |

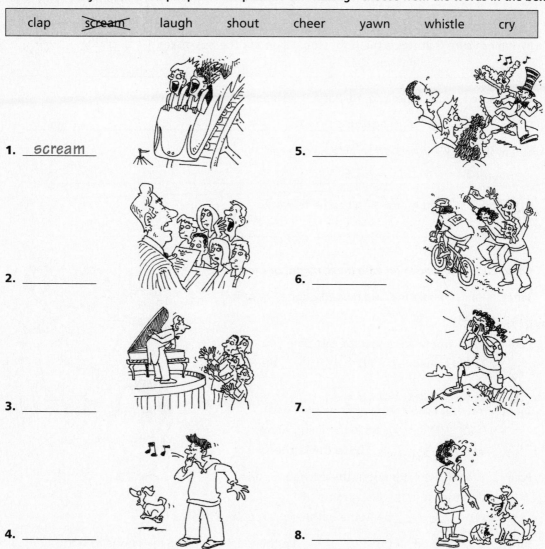

1. _scream_

2. _____

3. _____

4. _____

5. _____

6. _____

7. _____

8. _____

2 Complete the sentences with the correct form of the verbs in Exercise 1. (You won't need all the verbs.)

1. The fans _____cheered_____ when their team scored the winning goal.

2. Louise _____ when her brother jumped out and scared her.

3. I was so tired that I _____ all through my classes.

4. I _____ because the movie had a very sad ending.

5. Everyone stood up and _____ at the end of the play.

6. I know it's not funny, but every time I see my dog chasing the mail carrier, I have to _____ .

57

Grammar

3 Rewrite the first sentence with *must be*, *might be*, or *can't be*.

1. I'm sure she isn't over 60 years old. She goes running every day.

She _can't be over 60 years old._

2. I'm sure she's Australian. That's what her accent sounds like.

She _____

3. I'm not sure that this is the right stop. I'll go ask the bus driver.

This _____

4. I'm sure he isn't American. He has a British accent.

He _____

5. I'm sure Jackie is rich. What an amazing car!

Jackie _____

6. Is Chuck sick today? He didn't come to work.

Chuck _____

4 Complete the conversation with *must*, *might*, or *can't*.

Janet: Can you help me find my cell phone? I lost it again!

Paul: Well, where were you the last time you called someone? It **(1)** ___must___ be there.

Janet: Yes, but I can't remember where I was! It **(2)** _____ be in the living room, or it **(3)** _____ be in the kitchen.

Paul: Hmmm, well, it's not in the kitchen . . . and I don't see it in the living room. It **(4)** _____ be in the bathroom. You're in there a lot.

Janet: Oh, come on. It **(5)** _____ be there. I never bring my phone into the bathroom.

Paul: Well, the only places we haven't looked are the bathroom and the garage, so it **(6)** _____ be one of those places.

Janet: You're so logical . . . OK, you look in the garage and I'll look in the bathroom, but I know it's not there!

Paul: Wait! I know . . . I'll call you and when the phone rings, we'll know where it is.

Janet: Great idea. Oh! It's really loud. It **(7)** _____ be very close.

Paul: It sure is. It's in your pocket!

Listening

5 🎧 **Play track 33. Listen to the sounds and check (✓) the ones Maria hears.**

1. coins dropping __✓__

2. traffic noise _____

3. cheering _____

4. someone shouting _____

5. clapping _____

6. people walking _____

6 🎧 **Play track 33 again. Circle the letter of the expressions you hear.**

1. ⓐ The person might work in a train station.

   b. The person must work in a train station.

2. **a.** He must be in a car.

   b. He might be in a car.

3. **a.** He can be a taxi driver.

   b. He can't be a taxi driver.

4. **a.** The person must be a bus driver.

   b. The person might be a bus driver.

Pronunciation

7 🎧 **Play track 34. Notice the weak pronunciation of the modals. Fill in the blanks in the sentences.**

1. He ___might___ be at an airport.

2. He _____ be a taxi driver.

3. He _____ be a bus driver.

4. She _____ be British.

5. No, she _____ be.

6. Then she _____ be Australian.

8 🎧 **Play track 34 again. Look at the words you wrote in the blanks. Draw a slash (/) through the /t/ sounds you don't hear clearly.**

9 🎧 **Play track 34 again. Listen and repeat.**

Mumbai Soap

Vocabulary

1 Complete the crossword puzzle.

Across

2 What you earn by working, and use in order to buy things

4 The ability to control people or events

6 Sickness or disease

7 The end of a person's or an animal's life

Down

1 Illegal activity

2 The relationship between two people who are husband and wife

3 A relationship between two unmarried people who love each other

5 The strong desire to have more money or possessions than you need

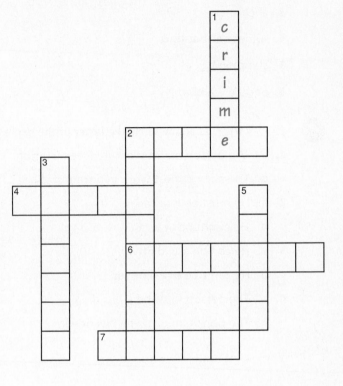

2 Complete the paragraph with the words from Exercise 1.

⬛ **TV Update** ⬛

City Nights is an exciting new soap opera about work, love, and death in the big city. In the opening episode, Bob and Laura's **(1)** marriage is falling apart and they are heading toward divorce. They are very wealthy, but all of their problems come from arguments about how to spend their **(2)** _____. Laura is motivated by **(3)** _____ and never feels satisfied with the money they have. Bob knows that money is **(4)** _____ and he wants to spend it so he can control people. The plot is complicated by the fact that Laura is suffering from a mysterious **(5)** _____ that makes her forget who she is. To make things more complicated, Laura thinks that Bob is having a **(6)** _____ with a girlfriend he used to have. Be sure to tune in this Wednesday at 3:00 when Laura forgets who she is, gets lost in a gambling casino, and gets involved with a group of gangsters who are about to commit a very serious **(7)** _____.

60

Grammar

3 Use *will/won't* and the verbs in the box to complete the horoscope. Use each verb only once.

be	fall	feel	have	love
make	~~move~~	need	notice	worry

What will the future bring?   Read your horoscope and find out!

Your stars **(1)** _will move_ into the best position possible and you **(2)**_____very lucky next month. You **(3)**_____ any problems. You **(4)**_____ in love with a wonderful, kind stranger and this person **(5)**_____ you in return. You **(6)**_____ lots of money and you **(7)**_____ about anything. You **(8)**_____ more and more confident. However, you **(9)**_____ a lot of non-verbal communication at work. You **(10)**_____ to listen not only with your ears, but also with your eyes and heart. All in all, this looks like a wonderful month for you.

4 Look at the fortune teller's predictions. Write to a friend about what the fortune teller thinks will happen to you.

You'll quit your job and move to Paris.

You'll meet someone there and fall in love.

You won't be happy in your job.

You'll return home alone.

You'll get a job in Atlanta.

You won't see each other for six months.

You'll never be happy until you see each other again.

The fortune teller . . .

1. _thinks I'll get a job in Atlanta._____.

2. _____.

3. _____.

4. _____.

5. _____.

6. _____.

7. _____.

15

Listening 🔊

5 🎧 **Play track 35. Number the events in the "Mumbai Soap" episode in the correct order.**

Nina emails Sanjay. _____

Nina's parents tell her to go to London. _____

Nina meets Sanjay at a soccer game in Mumbai. __1__

Sanjay tells Nina that she should forget him. _____

Ravi asks Nina to marry him. _____

Nina gets an offer to work in a soap opera. _____

6 🎧 **Play track 35 again. Check (✓) the correct sentences.**

1. a. Nina's parents think she will forget Sanjay. __✓__

   b. Nina's parents don't think she will forget Sanjay. _____

2. a. Nina doesn't think she will see Sanjay again. _____

   b. Nina thinks she will see Sanjay again. _____

3. a. Nina and Ravi will get married soon. _____

   b. Nina and Ravi won't get married soon. _____

4. a. Sanjay thinks Nina will be happier without him. _____

   b. Nina thinks Sanjay will be happier without her. _____

Pronunciation 🔊

7 🎧 **Play track 71. Notice the pronunciation of the contracted and weak forms of *will*. Fill in the blanks.**

1. ____I'll____ always love you.

2. _____ forget me.

3. _____ go to London.

4. I think _____ get married.

5. Do you think _____ be too late?

6. She _____ marry someone else.

7. She thinks her heart _____ break.

8 🎧 **Play track 71 again. Listen and repeat.**

The message behind the ad

Vocabulary

1 Cross out the adjective that does not usually go with the noun.

1.
fast / safe

2.
delicious / soft

3.
fast / shiny

4.
fast / healthy

5.
reliable / fresh

6.
reliable / soft

2 Complete the conversations with words from Exercise 1.

1. **Laura:** Why do you go to all the trouble to squeeze your orange juice every morning?

   Karen: Because I want the very best-tasting orange juice I can get.

   Laura: Mmmmm . . . I see what you mean. It sure is ___delicious___.

2. **Wayne:** How do you like your new computer?

   Carlos: It's fantastic. I got a satellite connection too, so it's really _____.

3. **Diana:** You make the best coffee! How do you do it?

   Rudy: I buy beans every day from the coffee roaster next door. It's really important to have _____ coffee beans.

4. **Joyce:** I love this new shampoo.

   Miranda: Me, too. Since I began to use it, my hair always looks _____ and soft.

5. **Noah:** Hey Matt, don't you think it's time to get a new car?

   Matt: Why should I? This one is old, but it never breaks down. It's the most _____ car I've ever had.

6. **Wanda:** Oh no, I got a sunburn again!

   Larry: You should put on some sunscreen — it's not _____ to get a sunburn like that.

Grammar

3 Complete the conversations with the present real conditional.

1. **A:** What she (do) if she (get) sick? <u>What will she do if she gets sick?</u>

   B: If she (get) sick, she (cancel) her trip. <u>If she gets sick, she'll cancel her trip.</u>

2. **A:** What (happen) if she (lose) her passport? _____

   B: If she (lose) her passport, she (go) to the Embassy. _____

3. **A:** If Jack (be) late, you (get) angry? _____

   B: No, but if he (not call) me, I (not wait) for him. _____

4. **A:** If Nancy's car (not start), what she (do)? _____

   B: She (call) us if that (happen). _____

5. **A:** If Pat (ask) you to come to her party, you (go)? _____

   B: Yes. And if I (go), you (come) with me? _____

4 Complete the advice with the appropriate form of the verb pairs in the box.

be / rinse	go away / change	~~not rest / get~~	not get / be
take / feel	not be able / drink	not study / fail	lose weight / eat

When you need good advice fast, ASK FRANCES

1. **Tom:** I'm getting a cold, but I can't take time off from work.

   Frances: If you ___<u>don't rest</u>___, your cold ___<u>will get</u>___ worse.

2. **Dan:** My roommates Frank and Ernest hate to study.

   Frances: If they _____ more, they _____ the class.

3. **Elizabeth:** I love coffee, but I have a hard time falling asleep at night.

   Frances: You _____ to sleep if you _____ too much coffee.

4. **Jeanette:** I really don't like my hair. I don't know what to do with it.

   Frances: Your hair _____ soft and shiny if you _____ it with lemon juice.

5. **Bill:** My daughter Betsy hates to go to bed.

   Frances: If she _____ enough sleep, she _____ very grumpy — and so will you.

6. **Deborah:** My boyfriend wants to lose weight, but he still wants to eat a lot.

   Frances: Tell him _____ if he _____ only fruit and vegetables.

7. **Larry:** I get really bad headaches all the time, but aspirin makes my stomach hurt.

   Frances: Some headaches _____ if you _____ your diet.

8. **Susan:** I get really nervous when I have to talk in front of people.

   Frances: If you _____ ten slow, deep breaths, you _____ much more relaxed.

Listening

5 ⌾ **Play track 37. Listen to the interview with the advertising executive. Check the products that are mentioned.**

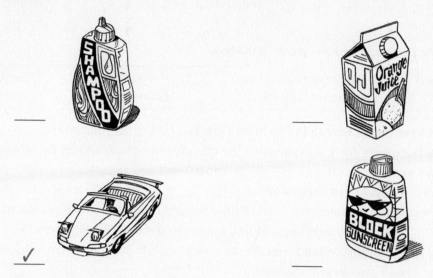

6 ⌾ **Play track 37 again. Complete the sentences with what the people say.**

1. If you __buy__ this car, you __'ll meet__ a beautiful woman.

2. If you _____ our product, you _____ it.

3. Your kids _____ sunburned if you _____ this sunscreen.

4. People _____ an ad if it _____ funny.

Pronunciation

7 ⌾ **Play track 38. Notice the stressed words in the *if* clause and the result clause. Underline these two words in each sentence.**

1. If you buy this <u>car,</u> you'll meet a beautiful <u>woman.</u>

2. If the ad is funny, people will remember it.

3. If you use this sunscreen, your kids won't get sunburned.

4. If you try our product, you won't regret it.

8 ⌾ **Play track 38 again. Listen and repeat.**

Self-Quiz for Units 13–16

Vocabulary

UNIT 13

A Complete the paragraph with the words in the box.

green card	ID (identification) card	immigration	nationalities
passport	permanent resident	~~tourist visa~~	work permit

Well, I'm in New York. It's great. I came in on a **(1)** _tourist visa_ . Some **(2)** _____
need a visa, but others don't. It depends on the country of origin. I can stay for 90 days, and
then I'll have to go to the **(3)** _____ department and apply for an extension. If I
want to work, I know I need to get a **(4)** _____. If I really like it here, I might decide
to live and work here permanently. Then I'll have to go through the whole process of getting
a **(5)** _____. They aren't easy to get, but once I get it, I'll be considered a
(6) _____ of the United States. That's a long way off. Right now, I'm not sure how
long I'll stay. I hope you can visit me here.

UNIT 14

B Match the beginnings of the sentences on the left with the endings on the right.

1. The man was yawning because __f__
2. The children were crying _____
3. The crowd was cheering loudly _____
4. The audience was screaming _____
5. The family was laughing at _____
6. It was so noisy, the woman was shouting _____

   a. during the horror film.
   b. as the winner crossed the finish line.
   c. the comedy program on TV.
   d. so that her friend could hear her.
   e. after they dropped their ice cream.
   f. he was very tired.

UNIT 15

C Underline the words that correctly complete the story.

In the last episode of "Our Lives," Mario lost his job. He is worried about not having enough
(1) power / money. To add to his **(2) misfortune / romance**, his best friend, Matt, is seriously ill,
and Matt's possible **(3) marriage / death** hangs over Mario. What's worse in his **(4) crime / family
life**, his wife, Tiffany, hasn't been home at all. He is worried that his **(5) marriage / power** is in
trouble. She says she's just late, but he thinks she's having a **(6) romance / greed**.

UNIT 16

D Match the sentences on the left with the responses on the right.

1. Have you tried this orange juice? __c__
2. Do you know of a good sunscreen? _____
3. What do you think of that shampoo? _____
4. My laptop keeps getting stuck! _____
5. How's the coffee? _____
6. I need a new laundry soap. _____

   a. I love it! It gives you healthy shiny hair!
   b. It's delicious. Can I have another cup?
   c. Yes, it's so fresh and sweet!
   d. This one makes your clothes soft and clean.
   e. Maybe you need something faster.
   f. This one is reliable, even in the water!

Grammar

UNIT 13

A Use the correct form of the verb in parentheses, or *for* or *since* to complete the story about Eva.

Eva was born in Brazil, but she **(1)** <u>has lived</u> **(live)** in the United States **(2)** _____ she was a little girl. She **(3)** _____ **(move)** to Boston with her parents twenty years ago. Her father **(4)** _____ **(work)** at a hotel **(5)** _____ a long time. Her mother **(6)** _____ **(go)** to school **(7)** _____ 2002 to become a nurse. Eva **(8)** _____ **(start)** working part time at a restaurant last July. **(9)** _____ then, she **(10)** _____ **(save)** a lot of money for college.

UNIT 14

B Complete the sentences with *must be, might be,* or *can't be.*

1. You worked until midnight? You <u>must be</u> exhausted today!

2. The baby _____ hungry again— I just fed him!

3. Rob's plane _____ a little late. He hasn't called from the airport.

4. Joanna _____ very happy about her new job.

5. The phone's ringing. It _____ my sister. She promised to call by 8:00.

6. It _____ hard to get tickets to that movie. Everyone wants to see it.

UNIT 15

C Wanda went to see a fortune teller. Write sentences about what the fortune teller thinks will and won't happen to Wanda.

You will move to New York.

You will get a job at a hotel.

You won't like the job because of the long hours.

You will meet someone special at the hotel.

You will get married and move to Spain.

Your family won't be happy about that.

1. <u>She thinks I'll move to New York.</u>   4. _____

2. _____   5. _____

3. _____   6. _____

UNIT 16

D Complete the sentences with the correct form of the verbs in parentheses.

1. If you ___<u>try</u>___ **(try)** this coffee, you <u>won't be</u> **(not be)** disappointed.

2. You _____ **(not get)** sunburned at the beach if you _____ **(use)** this sunscreen.

3. If you _____ **(drink)** this fresh orange juice, you _____ **(have)** lots of energy.

4. Your hair _____ **(look)** clean and shiny if you _____ **(use)** this shampoo.

5. If you _____ **(take)** the new express train, you _____ **(get)** to work much faster.

Willpower

Vocabulary

1 Complete each item on the list of New Year's resolutions with the correct verb from the box.
(One verb is used twice.)

cut	give	keep	take	throw	~~turn~~

New Year's Resolutions

1. Don't _turn_ down the chance to try new things!
2. _____ down on coffee.
3. _____ away old clothes.
4. _____ up Tai Chi classes.
5. _____ on exercising every morning.
6. _____ back on overtime at work.
7. _____ up chocolate.

2 Complete the conversation with the appropriate form of the phrasal verbs in Exercise 1.

Jill: Hi Carol. I didn't know you were interested in boxing!

Carol: Well, it's a new interest. I decided to **(1)** _____take up_____ boxing as one of my New Year's resolutions.

Jill: Really! Why boxing?

Carol: Well, I want to lose some weight.

Jill: Then why don't you just **(2)** _____ on sweets or **(3)** _____ on fatty foods?

Carol: That was my resolution last year, but I finally **(4)** _____ on the idea. I just don't have much willpower. It's really hard to **(5)** _____ sweets when someone offers you some.

Jill: Yeah, I know what you mean. When I was on a diet, I had to **(6)** _____ all the junk food in my house so I wouldn't be tempted to eat it.

Carol: Why don't you join my boxing class? That way we can burn a lot of calories and **(7)** _____ eating as much junk food as we want!

The art of crime

Vocabulary

1 Use the words in the box to write the name of the crime under each picture.

bank robbery	burglary	mugging	~~scam~~	shoplifting	theft

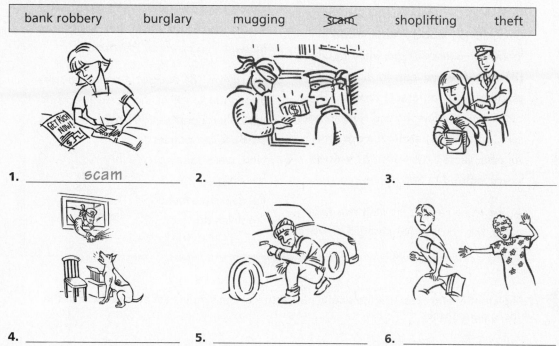

1. _____scam_____   2. _____   3. _____

4. _____   5. _____   6. _____

2 Complete the newspaper crime report with the correct form of the words in Exercise 1.

Criminal Activity on the Rise

There was another bank **(1)** _____robbery_____ last night. Police are asking for help in identifying the two masked men who **(2)** _____robbed_____ Central Bank around midnight. Police say that the **(3)** _____robbers_____ are dangerous.

In the past week, local store owners have reported over 50 cases of **(4)**_____ in their stores. About $1,000 in merchandise was taken from various stores. The only good news is that more and more of these **(5)**_____ are being caught.

Police are reminding citizens to always lock their cars. There was another car **(6)** _____ last night from the city center parking lot. Police are asking for help in tracking down the **(7)** _____ who stole a brand-new red sports car last night.

Police investigators thank local residents for their phone calls about the **(8)** _____ who was breaking into homes along Market Street last week. He is now in jail, and there have been no more **(9)** _____ reported.

Grammar

3 Circle the correct form of the verb.

On December 22, 2000, three armed robbers **(1)** ⟨walked⟩ / **were walked** into the lobby of the National Museum as it was closing. One thief **(2) stood / was stood** in the lobby with a machine gun while the others **(3) ran / were run** to three specific paintings in different rooms. Three paintings—two Renoirs and a Rembrandt self-portrait— **(4) stole / were stolen**. Together, these three works **(5) valued / were valued** at $60 million.

At the same time as the theft was taking place, two car fires **(6) started / were** **started** by accomplices in the museum parking lot, confusing police who responded to the security alarms. In the chaos, the three robbers **(7) escaped / were escaped** from the waterfront museum in a powerful speedboat.

The thieves **(8) caught / were caught** through luck, rather than detective work, when their apartment **(9) raided / was raided** by police who were looking for drugs. Instead, the detectives found the stolen art.

4 Complete the sentences. Use the simple past active or the simple past passive form of the verbs in parentheses.

1. Jack's radio ___was stolen___ (steal) from his car while he ____ate____ (eat) in a nearby restaurant.

2. The burglars _____ (give) light sentences because they _____ (turn) themselves in to the police and _____ (return) everything to their victims.

3. The shoplifters _____ (catch) immediately because the security guard _____ (call) by some customers.

4. The detective _____ (give) contradictory information, so he _____ (not trust) any of the witnesses.

5. The suspects _____ (tell) that they were free to go because the police _____ (not have) enough evidence against them.

Listening 🔊

5 🎧 **Play track 50. Listen to the story of the art theft and circle the correct answer for each question.**

1. Where can the Mona Lisa be seen?

    a. Rome

    (b.) Paris

    c. London

2. What happened to Vincenzo Perugia?

    a. He was arrested.

    b. He was offered the painting.

    c. He was paid for the painting.

3. What happened to the six copies of the Mona Lisa?

    a. They were destroyed by the police.

    b. They were sold to collectors.

    c. They were taken to the museum.

6 🎧 **Listen to track 50 again. Correct the verbs in each statement.**

painted

1. The Mona Lisa was ~~created~~ by Leonardo da Vinci.

2. In 1911, the painting was taken from the museum.

3. Two years later, it was sold to an art dealer in Florence.

4. In fact, the theft was carried out by a con artist called Eduardo de Valfierno.

5. The Mona Lisa was brought back to the Louvre.

Pronunciation 🔊

7 🎧 **Play track 51. Notice that the stressed syllable of each important word is long and clear. The unstressed syllables and unimportant words are short and weak. Underline the syllables with the main stress in each sentence.**

1. <u>How</u> were the <u>thieves</u> <u>caught</u>?

2. When was the painting stolen?

3. Copies of the painting were made.

4. The copies were sold to collectors.

5. The original was offered to a dealer.

6. The painting was returned to the museum.

8 🎧 **Play track 51 again. Listen and repeat.**

A balanced life

Vocabulary

1 Circle the correct word to complete the sentences.

1. Golf is OK, but I prefer taking **it easy** /(**part**)/ **a break** in team sports like basketball or soccer.

2. The coach told everyone to take **up** / **part** / **a break** for five minutes.

3. My son has a bad cold, so I took the day **on** / **up** /(**off**)to look after him.

4. You look tired. Why don't you sit down and take **off** / **up** / **it easy**?

5. I'm really out of shape. I think I'll take **on** / **off** /(**up**)jogging.

6. Her colleague is sick, so she's taking **off**/ **on** / **up** some of his work.

2 Rewrite the sentences. Use expressions with *take* to replace the underlined words.

1. I love Latin music, so I'm going to <u>begin</u> salsa dancing.

   <u>I love Latin music, so I'm going to take up</u>
   <u>salsa dancing.</u>

2. My wife says I <u>agree to do</u> too many extra jobs at work, but it's really hard to say no to my boss.

   Take on

3. Tomorrow Thomas and I are going to participate in a marathon to raise money for charity.

   take part

4. We don't have any plans for Saturday—we're just going to <u>relax</u>.

   take easy

5. I'm going to <u>arrange to have time away from work</u> so I can show my Brazilian friends around.   take off time from.

6. You've been working too hard lately. Why don't you stop and <u>have a rest</u>?
   take a break.

Grammar

3 Complete the sentences with the gerund or infinitive of the verbs from the box. If both the gerund and infinitive may be used, write them both. (Note: Some verbs can be used more than once.)

cook	go	play	study	wash	work

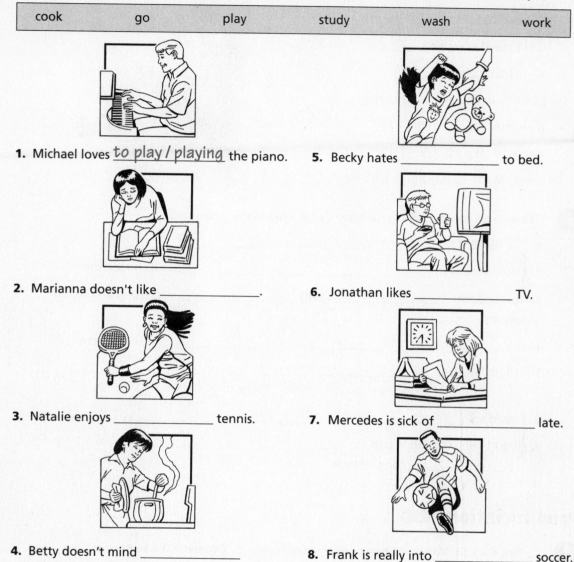

1. Michael loves *to play / playing* the piano.

2. Marianna doesn't like _____.

3. Natalie enjoys _____ tennis.

4. Betty doesn't mind _____ dinner for her family.

5. Becky hates _____ to bed.

6. Jonathan likes _____ TV.

7. Mercedes is sick of _____ late.

8. Frank is really into _____ soccer.

4 Find and correct four more errors in the diary entry.

> *doing*
> Usually I don't mind ~~to do~~ my homework, but last night I was so sick of do homework that I decided to go out with George. He enjoys to go to the movies, so I suggested a romantic comedy. But George said he hates romantic movies and suggested an action movie instead. But I can't stand seeing so much violence, so finally we decided seeing that new Japanese animated film. We both really enjoyed to watch it, and we had a wonderful time.

Listening 🔊

5 🎧 **Play track 52. Listen to the conversation between Marta and Ian. Check (✓) the reasons Ian gives for not wanting to go to the gym.**

Decided to take the evening off. __✓__

Can't stand exercising. _____

Wants time alone. _____

Sick of running around the gym. _____

Is already in good shape. _____

Needs to take a break. _____

Wants Marta to stay home with him. _____

6 🎧 **Play track 52 again. Fill in the blanks with what Marta or Ian said.**

1. I've decided to _____take_____ the evening _____off_____ .

2. I think I've been _____ _____ too much recently.

3. You said you _____ really _____ exercising and losing weight.

4. I'm _____ _____ _____ around the gym.

5. I think I've been _____ _____ _____

_____ .

6. I need to _____ _____ _____ .

7. I don't mind staying in and _____ _____

_____ for a change.

Pronunciation 🔊

7 🎧 **Play track 53. Notice the groups of consonant sounds. Complete the sentences.**

1. I _can't stand playing_ tennis, but I _____ swimming.

2. She _____ , but she _____ yoga.

3. He _____ , but _____ he

_____ to take a _____ .

8 🎧 **Play track 53 again. Listen and repeat.**

Digital age

Vocabulary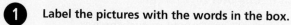

1 Label the pictures with the words in the box.

cell phone	computer	digital camera	~~digital TV~~
DVD player	laptop computer	printer	scanner

1. ____digital TV____
2. _____
3. _____
4. _____
5. _____
6. _____
7. _____
8. _____

1.
2.
3.
4.

5.
6.
7.
8.

2 Complete the sentences with words from Exercise 1.

1. ____Digital TV____ allows viewers to interact with the station.

2. A _____ has a built-in screen and keyboard and is easy to carry around.

3. The good thing about a _____ is that you can call people from almost anywhere.

4. A _____ can convert images or text on paper to digital images that you can manipulate in your computer.

5. You can take a picture with a _____ without using film.

6. Some are color and some are black and white, but all _____ let you make paper copies of things from your computer.

7. A _____ is like a CD player except that it produces video images, not just audio.

8. A _____ is an electronic machine that stores information and uses programs to help you find, organize, or change your information.

Grammar

3 Complete each sentence with *who, that, which,* or *where.* More than one answer is correct in some cases.

1. A device <u>that, which</u> takes pictures without using film is called a digital camera.

2. A person _____ programs computers is a computer programmer.

3. An Internet café is a place _____ you can check your email or surf the net.

4. Scanners are devices _____ transform images or text into digital information.

5. A video store is a place _____ you can rent videos or DVDs.

6. A person _____ makes sure people aren't stealing things from stores is called a security guard.

7. A book _____ has definitions of words is called a dictionary.

4 Read a report on technophobia. Find and correct six more mistakes in the relative pronouns. In some cases more than one relative pronoun may be correct.

                                                 which

I just read a book called **Technophobia**, ~~who~~ was written by Dr. Linda Smith, a psychologist and computer programmer. Dr. Smith says that the word "technophobia" was first used in 1978 in Silicon Valley, California, which many computer people work. Of course, people which work with computers don't understand "technophobes," the people which are afraid to use new technology.

    But I understand what Dr. Smith is writing about because I have a friend that is a technophobe. She is very intelligent, but she can't deal with technology.

    Dr. Smith says that technophobia is a problem who affects many people. It prevents them from using technology who could save them time and effort. But she also says technophobia is not hard to overcome. Dr. Smith gives many helpful tips in her book, who can be purchased from her website.

Listening

5 🎧 Play track 55. Complete the statements with the correct choice.

1. TV programs are the information sent from the studio to __*b*__.

   a. our offices   **b.** our homes   **c.** our sets

2. With digital TV, you can watch your favorite program and even _____ the station.

   a. vote on   **b.** play with   **c.** talk to

6 🎧 Play track 55 again. Complete the sentences.

1. A TV studio is a place _where they produce_ TV programs.

2. Digital TV systems only send _____ change.

3. But they send a lot of pictures _____ walking or cars _____ moving.

4. In areas _____ is available, you need either a special TV or _____ can put the pictures together for your non-digital TV.

Pronunciation

7 🎧 Play track 54. Notice the strongly stressed syllables in the words. Underline the stressed syllables in each word.

1. <u>cell</u> phone

2. computer

3. digital TV

4. DVD player

5. laptop

6. printer

7. remote control

8. scanner

8 🎧 Play track 54 again. Listen and repeat.

Self-Quiz for Units 21–24

Vocabulary

UNIT 21

A Complete the sentences with *on, off, up,* or *down*.

1. Please turn _____*on*_____ the light. It's too dark in here.

2. Would you mind turning _____ the air conditioner? It's freezing in here.

3. Could you please turn _____ the radio? I can't study with music playing.

4. Would you please turn _____ the computer so that I can check my email?

5. Would you please turn _____ the music so that we can hear it in the other room?

UNIT 22

B Write the correct form of the words under the headlines. Use *burglarize, mug, rob,* or *shoplift*.

1.
> Man Enters House and Takes Picasso Replica Worth $30

2.
> Teenagers Take 20 Beethoven CDs from Local Music Store

3.
> Armed Men Wearing Masks Leave Bank with $100,000

4.
> Man Hits Jogger with Banana, Takes Watch Worth $250

	Crime	Criminal	Verb
1	burglary	burglar	burglarize
2			
3			
4			

UNIT 23

C Complete the sentences with expressions with *take*. Use *it easy, a break, part in, on,* or *up*.

1. Do you want to take ___*part in*___ a road race in June? It's for charity—a really good cause.

2. Please don't take _____ more than you can handle.

3. After working hard all week, Les likes to take _____ on the weekend.

4. Let's take _____ and have some lunch. We can finish this later.

5. If you're interested in music, why don't you take _____ a musical instrument?

UNIT 24

D Complete the sentences with *cell phone, computer, digital camera, DVD player, laptop, printer,* or *scanner*. (You won't need all the words.)

1. My new ___*laptop*___ makes it easy for me to work on the train.

2. If you connect the new _____, we can watch a movie.

3. Can you lend me your _____ so that I can make a quick call?

4. My new _____ is great because I can take so many pictures with it.

5. If we had a _____, we could add this picture to our party invitation.

Grammar

UNIT 21

 A Write a polite request for each situation. Use the words in parentheses and *please*. Use a separate piece of paper.

1. You want your brother to turn down the TV a little. (**Could you**)

   Could you turn down the TV a little, please?

2. You want your classmate to lower his voice. (**Would you mind**)

3. You want your friend to lend you some money until tomorrow. (**Could you**)

4. You want to turn on the TV at your friend's house. (**Could I**)

5. Your neighbors' dog is barking, and you want them to take their dog inside. (**Would**)

UNIT 22

 B Rewrite the sentences in the passive. Don't mention the agent unless it's necessary. Use a separate piece of paper.

1. The car thieves stole six cars right off the car lot.

   Six cars were stolen right off the car lot.

2. The police caught the bank robber as he tried to run away.

3. Someone stole my new leather jacket from the backseat of my car.

4. Someone took Roberto's motorcycle last night from outside his apartment.

5. Video pirates made hundreds of copies of the movie.

UNIT 23

C Circle the verb form that correctly completes each sentence. If both are correct, circle both.

1. Joshua hates (**to go**) / (**going**) shopping for new shoes.

2. Sergio is sick of to **work / working** late on weekends.

3. Steve likes **to play / playing** hockey on his high school team.

4. Ericka doesn't mind **to wash / washing** the dishes after dinner.

5. Peter enjoys **to be / being** in a book club.

6. Amelia can't stand **to listen / listening** to jazz music.

UNIT 24

 D Read the letter. Find and correct five more mistakes with *who, which, that*, or *where*.

> Mr. Rodriguez,
>
>   *that*
>
>   We have a few equipment problems ~~who~~ I need to bring to your attention. First, we are having problems
>
> with our printer. The technician which usually does our repairs says he is behind schedule. We need someone
>
> where can fix it as soon as possible. Our other problem is the scanner where we use to make our brochures.
>
> It isn't working right, either. If you have someone in your department who you can send over, we would
>
> appreciate it. Finally, do you know a good place which we can buy an inexpensive digital camera? If there is
>
> someone in your office where is an expert, let us know.
>
> Regards,
>
> T. Withering

Arranged marriages

Vocabulary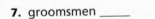

1 Match the pictures with the words.

1. groom __g__

2. reception _____

3. ceremony _____

4. bride _____

5. honeymoon _____

6. bridesmaids _____

7. groomsmen _____

8. best man _____

9. maid of honor _____

a.

b.

c.

d.

e.

f.

g.

h.

i.

2 Use the correct form of the verbs in the box to complete the ad for "Love in the City" in the TV schedule.

~~get engaged~~	get over	get divorced	get upset
get on each other's nerves	get along	get married	

Tonight's the Night?

There's a big wedding scheduled for tonight on **"Love in the City."** You'll remember that Celeste and William **(1)** _got engaged_ on the show three long years ago. And lately it seems like they don't **(2)** _____ as well as they used to. In fact, they **(3)** _____ all the time. Last week Celeste really **(4)** _____ when William stayed out all night with his friends. She is still angry and hasn't **(5)** _____ it, so she moved into her mother's house. Things are not looking good. Will Celeste and William finally **(6)** _____ and forget their problems? Will they **(7)** _____ afterwards because their problems just don't go away? Watch "Love in the City" at 8:00 and find out!

Grammar

3 Ross and Lorena have very different views of marriage. Fill in the blanks in their conversation using the cues and the phrase *it's . . . (for) to . . .*

Lorena: Hi Ross. Did you hear that Kevin and Maria are getting married?

Ross: Yes, but I'm not sure **(1)** <u>it's a good idea for people to get married</u> **(good idea / people to get married)** when they've only known each other for three months.

Lorena: Oh, come on. **(2)** _____ **(wonderful / people to get married)**, no matter how long they've known each other.

Ross: Time is important, you know. I really think **(3)** _____ **(bad idea / people to make rushed decisions)**.

Lorena: Really? Why?

Ross: **(4)** _____ **(crazy / think that you will get to know)** a person after a few months.

Lorena: I completely disagree. Don't you believe in love at first sight?

Ross: Oh, come on. **(5)** _____ **(wonderful / to fall in love)** immediately, but that's extremely rare. That only happens in movies. And **(6)** _____ **(absurd / anyone to think)** that you want to spend the rest of your life with the person you met five minutes ago.

Lorena: Well, I still think that **(7)** _____ **(not important / wait a long time)** to find out that you love someone.

4 Use the phrases in the box to rewrite the sentences so that they have the same meaning. Use each phrase once.

(not) important	(not) a good idea	(not) a bad idea
(not) crazy	(not) absurd	(not) wonderful

1. You should let your parents help you choose your spouse.

   <u>It's a good idea to let your parents help you choose your spouse.</u>

2. It's great news that Beth and Scott are getting married!

   _____

3. People shouldn't wait for "Mr. Right" or "Ms. Right" to come along.

   _____

4. You should know someone for at least three years before you get married.

   _____

5. Couples shouldn't abandon their friends after getting married.

   _____

6. It really doesn't matter if couples don't have the same hobbies and interests.

   _____

Listening

5 ∩ Play track 57. Listen to Monica and Carlos talk about marriage. Check (✓) all the words and phrases related to love and marriage that you hear.

wedding	✓	bride	_____
marriage	_____	best man	_____
get married	_____	groom	_____
husband	_____	get engaged	_____
wife	_____	get divorced	_____
love	_____	the married couple	_____

6 ∩ Play track 57 again. Complete the sentences with what the people say.

1. It's ___important for her to___ marry someone her parents like.

2. Maybe it's _____ let your parents arrange things.

3. It's _____ get married to someone you don't know.

4. In India, it's _____ to get along.

5. I still think it's _____ marry someone you've never met before.

Pronunciation

7 ∩ Play track 73. Notice the different pronunciations of /t/. Complete the sentences.

1. They went _____*out together*_____ for three years.

2. Sometimes they _____ each other's nerves.

3. They _____ know each other well.

4. But most of the time, they _____ well.

5. She _____ in September.

8 ∩ Play track 73 again. Listen and repeat.

Money matters

Vocabulary

1 Circle the correct phrase to complete the sentences.

1. Sorry, but I can't go out tonight. I just got my **bank statement** / **bank account**, and my balance is low. I really have to watch what I spend this month.

2. I always have money. I can **deposit money** / **withdraw money** from the ATM whenever I need it.

3. If you put your money in a savings account, you'll **receive interest** / **pay interest** every month.

4. Bad news. The company isn't hiring anyone new for the rest of the year because it's **in the red** / **in the black** again.

5. Here, I'll pay for the pizza. I just **borrowed** / **lent** $20 from my dad.

2 Complete the conversations with the words in the box.

borrowed	checking	deposit	in the black	interest
lend	~~saving~~	savings	statement	withdrawing

I'm **(1)** __saving__ all I can for my retirement. I've never **(2)** _____ any money—from my friends or my bank. I think if you can't pay for something, you shouldn't buy it. Every month, I **(3)** _____ money I know I'm not going to spend into my **(4)** _____ account. You know it's safe there, and the bank pays me **(5)** _____, about 5 percent a year. It all adds up over time, you know.

I think you should enjoy life and spend your money while you can. I'm always **(6)** _____ money from my **(7)** _____ account—I never know how much money I have until the bank sends me a **(8)** _____. I'm always asking people to **(9)** _____ me money to get back **(10)** _____. It doesn't worry me though—after all, it's only money!

Grammar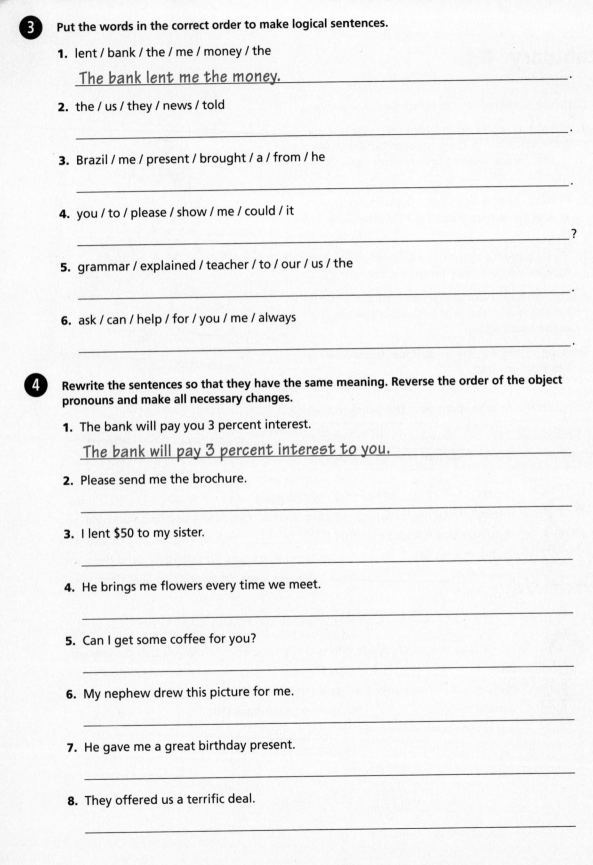

3 Put the words in the correct order to make logical sentences.

1. lent / bank / the / me / money / the

_The bank lent me the money._____.

2. the / us / they / news / told

_____.

3. Brazil / me / present / brought / a / from / he

_____.

4. you / to / please / show / me / could / it

_____?

5. grammar / explained / teacher / to / our / us / the

_____.

6. ask / can / help / for / you / me / always

_____.

4 Rewrite the sentences so that they have the same meaning. Reverse the order of the object pronouns and make all necessary changes.

1. The bank will pay you 3 percent interest.

_The bank will pay 3 percent interest to you._____

2. Please send me the brochure.

_____

3. I lent $50 to my sister.

_____

4. He brings me flowers every time we meet.

_____

5. Can I get some coffee for you?

_____

6. My nephew drew this picture for me.

_____

7. He gave me a great birthday present.

_____

8. They offered us a terrific deal.

_____

Listening

5 Play track 58. Listen to the first part of an advertisement for DirBanking. Number the pictures in the order of the questions about them.

_____

_____

_1_

6 Play track 58 again. Listen to the second part of the advertisement. Complete the ad about the bank's services.

Here at DirBanking, we save you time and money. You can access your account 24 hours a day, seven days a week.

- We **(1)** _____provide_____ full banking services **(2)** _____to you_____ through your telephone, computer, or cell phone.

- We can **(3)** _____ money at the best interest rates.

- We can **(4)** _____ advice on buying and selling stocks online.

- We **(5)** _____ financial security **(6)** _____.

- We **(7)** _____ first-class service.

- We **(8)** _____ peace of mind.

Remember: DirBanking **(9)** _____ first-class banking — direct to you, wherever you are.

Pronunciation

7 Play track 59. Notice the weak pronunciation of the object pronouns. Complete the sentences with the correct pronouns.

1. He sent _____me_____ a bill.

2. They owe _____ money.

3. I can lend _____ some money.

4. We sent _____ a check.

5. I gave _____ a receipt.

6. Did you buy _____ a present?

8 Play track 59 again. Listen and repeat.

Less is more

Vocabulary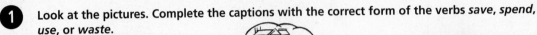

1 Look at the pictures. Complete the captions with the correct form of the verbs *save*, *spend*, *use*, or *waste*.

1. They say that the U.S. _____ uses _____ more resources per person than any other country.

2. We're trying to _____ money to buy a house.

3. Why do companies _____ so much paper on junk mail?

4. Let's take the expressway. We'll _____ 15 minutes if we don't have to wait for traffic lights.

5. Unfortunately, I can't _____ more than $25 on this birthday present.

6. My kid uses the Internet to do his research papers, but I think he _____ a lot of time now just chatting.

2 Complete the article with the words in the box.

save your energy	using your time	wasting time
~~spend some time~~	save you time	waste of energy

HURRY SICKNESS

Many business people are suffering from a 21st-century epidemic — "Hurry Sickness." They try to fit *everything* into *every* day. They can't seem to do it all, so they're always stressed out. To avoid hurry sickness, follow these tips:

1. _Spend some time_ planning your day before you start your workday.

2. Don't get impatient if your computer is slow. _____ for the more important things in life.

3. Realize that taking breaks is _____ well.

4. Going out for lunch instead of eating at your desk is not _____.

5. Getting angry about traffic on your way to work is a _____. It doesn't _____ or get you there faster.

Grammar

3 Put the words in the right order to give advice to someone who is feeling stressed out.

1. more / take / you / breaks / should

<u>You should take more breaks.</u>

2. breaths / try / you / taking / could / deep / ten

_____

3. not / at / lunch / your / should / desk / you / eat

_____

4. do / ought / exercise / to / day / you / some / every

_____

5. walk / take / you / outdoors / could / a

_____

6. go / you / with / to / dinner / should / a / friend / out

_____

7. refuse / overtime / could / to / you / work

_____

4 Karen is giving advice to her friend. Find and correct five more mistakes in her email.

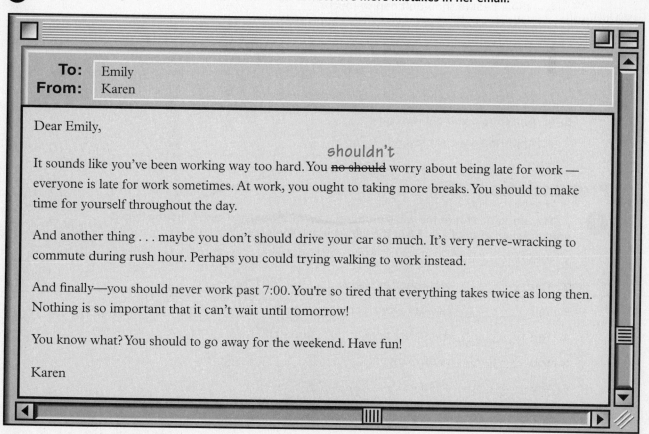

To: Emily
From: Karen

Dear Emily,

It sounds like you've been working way too hard. You ~~no should~~ *shouldn't* worry about being late for work — everyone is late for work sometimes. At work, you ought to taking more breaks. You should to make time for yourself throughout the day.

And another thing . . . maybe you don't should drive your car so much. It's very nerve-wracking to commute during rush hour. Perhaps you could trying walking to work instead.

And finally—you should never work past 7:00. You're so tired that everything takes twice as long then. Nothing is so important that it can't wait until tomorrow!

You know what? You should to go away for the weekend. Have fun!

Karen

Listening

5 Play track 60. Listen to the interview with author Laura Chang. Number the pictures in the order the topics are mentioned.

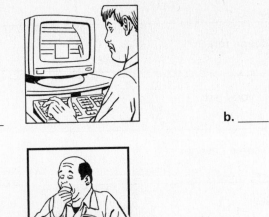

a. _____

b. _____

c. _____

d. __1__

6 Play track 60 again. Check (✓) the sentences you hear.

1. a. I say we should work longer hours. _____

   b. I say we should work shorter hours. __✓__

2. a. I think people shouldn't sleep so much. _____

   b. I think people shouldn't nap so much. _____

3. a. We shouldn't forget that technology is for saving money. _____

   b. We shouldn't forget that technology is for saving energy. _____

4. a. We should all spend less time at the computer. _____

   b. We should all spend less time at the cafeteria. _____

5. a. And should you eat less, too? _____

   b. And should we eat less, too? _____

Pronunciation

7 Play track 61. Notice the weak pronunciation of *should* and *could* and the linked pronunciation of *ought to*. Fill in the blanks in the sentences.

1. What __should__ I do?

2. You _____ work shorter hours.

3. You _____ take an afternoon nap.

4. You _____ spend less time at the computer.

5. You _____ relax more.

6. You _____ sleep less.

8 Play track 61 again. Listen and repeat.

Celebrate

Vocabulary

1 Circle the word in each group that doesn't belong.

1. (potluck dinner)	pianist	live music	black tie dinner
2. pianist	family reunion	anniversary	wedding
3. dinner	DJ	barbecue	potluck dinner
4. live music	DJ	pianist	dinner
5. birthday	anniversary	live music	graduation

2 Complete the sentences with words from Exercise 1.

1. It was a very elegant wedding reception. The _____*pianist*_____ played Mozart concertos.

2. I love summer because we get to cook outdoors—there's nothing like a _____!

3. My sister and her husband have been married for ten years on Sunday, so we're taking them out for a special _____ dinner.

4. Let's have a _____ and ask everyone to bring their favorite dish.

5. Jack finishes college in May, so we're going to have a huge _____ party the first weekend of June.

6. We can't afford live music at the party, so we'll just hire a _____.

Grammar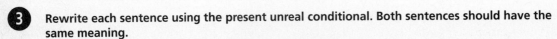

3 Rewrite each sentence using the present unreal conditional. Both sentences should have the same meaning.

1. I don't know his phone number, so I can't call him.

   If I knew his phone number, I'd call him.

2. She can't eat out tonight because she doesn't have enough money.

   _____

3. Kim doesn't study very hard, so she won't pass her exam.

   _____

4. Jason doesn't exercise, so he's not in very good shape.

   _____

5. I can't go to the gym tonight because I'm really tired.

   _____

6. I don't have my credit card with me, so I can't buy the jacket.

   _____

4 Use the cues to write sentences about what David would like to do.

have three weeks off → take a trip to Korea

1. *If he had three weeks off, he would take a trip to Korea.*

have a sailboat → go sailing every weekend

2. _____

live in the country → buy a horse

3. _____

get a salary increase → be very happy

4. _____

106

Listening 🔊

5 🎧 Play track 62. Listen to the first part of the radio advertisement for a magazine competition. Answer the questions.

1. What is the magazine celebrating?

   <u>They are celebrating their 100th edition.</u>

2. What can you win?

   _____

3. What will the sponsors pay for?

   _____

6 🎧 Play track 62 again. Listen to the second part of the radio advertisement. Complete the questions.

1. <u>Who would it</u> be for?

2. _____ have the party?

3. _____ celebrate?

4. _____ type of party _____ it be?

5. _____ have the party?

6. _____ food and drink _____ you choose?

7. _____ people _____ invite?

Pronunciation 🔊

7 🎧 Play track 63. Notice the pronunciation of the weak and contracted forms of *would*. Fill in the blanks.

1. Where _____<u>would</u>_____ it be?

2. If you could have a party, where _____ it be?

3. _____ have the party at a restaurant.

4. I _____ cook.

5. _____ have live music.

6. _____ play salsa.

7. _____ dance all night.

8. Everyone _____ have a great time.

8 🎧 Play track 63 again. Listen and repeat.

Self-Quiz for Units 25–28

Vocabulary

UNIT 25

A Complete the paragraph with the words in the box.

best man	bride	bridesmaids	~~groom~~	groomsmen	maid of honor

On Saturday, Luis Mendoza and Teresa Sanchez were married at the Eastwinds Country Club.
The **(1)** __groom__, Luis, was attended by his brother, who was his **(2)** _____. The
(3) _____, Teresa, was attended by four _____, and her sister, who was the
(5) _____. There were also four **(6)** _____, who were Luis's brothers and close
friends from his soccer team. All of the members of the wedding party knew one another well.

UNIT 26

B Complete the sentences with the words in the box. (You won't need all the words.)

borrow	deposit	~~in the black~~	in the red	lend	pay back	save	withdraw

1. Ruth was tired of owing money. She wanted to be __in the black__ again.
2. Tracey got a job to _____ the money she borrowed from her parents.
3. Can you _____ me some money for lunch? I left my wallet at the office.
4. Remind me to stop at the bank. I need to _____ my paycheck.
5. My brother tries to _____ money every month so that he can buy a new car.

UNIT 27

C Complete the sentences with *use, waste, spend,* or *save.*

1. Henry tries to ___spend___ at least an hour at the gym every other day.
2. We're going to stop eating out so much so we can _____ money for a trip to Europe.
3. The environmental plan helped the community _____ its resources better.
4. Please turn off the lights when you leave the room so that we don't _____ electricity.
5. Don't worry about the trip. _____ your time thinking about relaxing!

UNIT 28

D Complete the sentences with the words in the box. (You won't need all the words.)

anniversary	birthday	black-tie dinner	~~DJ~~	family reunion	graduation	potluck	wedding

1. We couldn't afford a live band, so we hired a ___DJ___ instead.
2. After the _____, the couple left for their honeymoon in Thailand.
3. We are going to throw a big _____ party for my brother when he finishes high school.
4. My grandparents wanted to have a big party to celebrate their 50th _____.
5. The _____ was a lot of fun. It was so great to see relatives I hadn't seen in years!

Grammar

UNIT 25

A Put the words in the correct order to write sentences. Add capital letters and punctuation where needed. Use a separate piece of paper.

1. not / ignore / it's / family's / a / idea / him his / advice / to / good / for

   It's not a good idea for him to ignore his family's advice.

2. someone / her same / it's / to / from / to / marry / important / the country

3. for / it's / him / finish / before / gets married / important / school / he / to

4. get married / meet / for / couples / to / after / they / crazy / it's / right

5. good / parents' / a / idea / listen / to / it's / opinions / your / to

6. couples / financial obligations / for / discuss / it's / getting married / important / before / to

UNIT 26

B Rewrite the sentences. Change the order of the direct and indirect objects. Use a separate piece of paper.

1. Would you mind lending me five dollars? *Would you mind lending five dollars to me?*

2. Could you please send us a copy of your last bank statement?

3. We now offer direct deposit to all full-time employees.

4. The sales associate forgot to give a receipt to me.

5. Have you bought them a wedding present yet?

6. The bank lent the money to our family to start a new business.

UNIT 27

C Read the list of ways to save energy. Rewrite each suggestion using the word in parentheses.

Ways to $AVE Energy at Home

1. It's a good idea to turn down your heat at night. **(should)**

2. Use fluorescent light bulbs in busy areas like the kitchen or bathroom. **(ought to)**

3. Put your computer on "sleep mode" when you aren't using it. **(could)**

4. Set your thermostat for your heat or air conditioning on a timer. **(ought to)**

5. Use solar-powered lights outside your home. **(could)**

6. In the summer, use curtains or shades to keep out the sunlight. **(should)**

1. *You should turn down your heat at night.*

UNIT 28

D Howie is day dreaming. Use the cues to write sentences about what he thinks he would like to do. Use a separate piece of paper.

1. have a car / drive to work   *If he had a car, he would drive to work.*

2. win the lottery / have a huge party

3. have a private airplane / take trips on the weekend

4. get a better job / move to a nicer apartment

5. have a lot of money / buy a race car

6. have a beach house / invite friends to visit

Self-Quiz Answer Key

UNITS 1–4
Vocabulary
Exercise A
a. 3
b. 5
c. 2
d. 4
e. 1
f. 6

Exercise B
1. hardworking
2. messy
3. noisy
4. talkative
5. cooperative
6. emotional

Exercise C
1. fitness center
2. swimming pool
3. conference rooms
4. business center
5. lobby
6. shuttle service
7. restaurants

Exercise D
1. I have a stomachache.
2. I have a backache.
3. I have a sore throat.
4. I have an earache.
5. I have a headache.
6. I have a rash.

Grammar
Exercise A
1. is working
2. needs
3. want
4. are thinking
5. looks
6. is doing

Exercise B
1. Juan isn't as talkative as Daniel.
2. Juan is more competitive than Daniel.
3. Anna is neater than Teresa.
4. Steve isn't as tall as Bob.
5. Toshi isn't as good at math as Keiko.
6. Jon is more emotional than Pedro.

Exercise C
1. Do you have
2. don't have
3. Do you want
4. doesn't have
5. don't need
6. does the deluxe double cost
7. doesn't include

Exercise D
1. surprised
2. annoying
3. frightened
4. disappointed
5. boring, bored
6. interested

UNITS 5–8
Vocabulary
Exercise A
1. send
2. pay
3. take out
4. make
5. take
6. spend

Exercise B
1. c
2. d
3. f
4. e
5. b
6. a

Exercise C
1. bland
2. polite
3. casual
4. sour
5. elegant
6. healthful

Exercise D
1. b
2. f
3. d
4. e
5. c
6. a

Grammar
Exercise A
1. Who usually cooks dinner?
2. Who does Raj almost always eat dinner with?
3. Who gets up at 6:00 A.M.?
4. Who does Sylvia spend her free time with?
5. Who is often late to class?
6. Who does Dan irritate when he comes to work late?

Exercise B
1. was waiting, saw
2. was walking, started
3. was opening, heard
4. was snowing, arrived
5. ate, got

Exercise C
1. The customer was too demanding.
2. The coffee wasn't hot enough for me.
3. That Italian restaurant is too noisy for a lunch-time meeting.
4. There aren't enough low-fat foods on this menu.
5. The tomato soup was too salty for us.
6. The chocolate dessert was too sweet for him.

Exercise D
1. have to
2. can't

3. don't have to
4. can't
5. have to/must
6. have to
7. can't

UNITS 9–12
Vocabulary
Exercise A
1. e
2. f
3. d
4. b
5. c
6. a

Exercise B
1. no trouble, simple
2. complicated, tough
3. doable, manageable

Exercise C
1. drapes
2. rug
3. throw pillows
4. lamp
5. picture
6. basket

Exercise D
1. at
2. in
3. at
4. no preposition
5. in
6. no preposition

Grammar
Exercise A
1. is coming
2. Is Shari arriving
3. is meeting
4. are going
5. are you doing
6. closes

Exercise B
1. Ravi was able to play tennis very well when he was in high school.
2. She never manages to pay her bills on time.
3. It rained all day, and so we couldn't take a walk.
4. The project was very demanding, but we were able to finish it on time.
5. The soccer player was able to kick the ball skillfully with either foot.
6. The young snowboarder can do many difficult tricks without falling.

Exercise C
1. has replaced
2. 've/have changed
3. has done
4. have hung
5. has saved
6. has decided

Exercise D
1. could
2. couldn't
3. may/might
4. may/might/could
5. might not/may not
6. may/might/could

UNITS 13–16
Vocabulary
Exercise A
1. tourist visa
2. nationalities
3. immigration
4. work permit
5. green card
6. permanent resident

Exercise B
1. f
2. e
3. b
4. a
5. c
6. d

Exercise C
1. money
2. misfortune
3. death
4. family life
5. marriage
6. romance

Exercise D
1. c
2. f
3. a
4. e
5. b
6. d

Grammar
Exercise A
1. has lived
2. since
3. moved
4. has worked
5. for
6. has gone
7. since
8. started
9. Since
10. has saved

Exercise B
1. must be
2. can't be
3. must/might be
4. must be
5. must/might be
6. might be

Exercise C

1. She thinks I'll move to New York.
2. She thinks I'll get a job at a hotel.
3. She doesn't think I'll like the job because of the long hours.
4. She thinks I'll meet someone special at the hotel.
5. She thinks I'll get married and move to Spain.
6. She doesn't think my family will be happy about that.

Exercise D

1. try, won't be
2. won't get, use
3. drink, will have
4. will look, use
5. take, will get

UNITS 17–20
Vocabulary
Exercise A

1. c
2. f
3. d
4. b
5. a
6. e

Exercise B

1. e
2. f
3. a
4. b
5. c

Exercise C

1. leather
2. wood
3. cotton
4. pewter
5. lycra
6. glass

Exercise D

1. martial arts film
2. horror movie
3. science fiction movie
4. comedy
5. action movie
6. drama

Grammar
Exercise A

1. to make
2. exercising
3. to join
4. to lose
5. to feel
6. drinking

Exercise B

1. used to have
2. would bother
3. would hide
4. used to live
5. used to be
6. would sneeze

Exercise C

1. Those wooden boxes are made by hand in Thailand.
2. Large quantities of excellent coffee are exported from Indonesia.
3. Some of the best chocolate in the world is produced by Belgium.
4. Do you know where this perfume is made?
5. A lot of soccer balls are made in Pakistan.
6. Some Japanese cars are made in the United States.

Exercise D

1. so have
2. neither did
3. so does
4. is too
5. shouldn't either
6. neither will

UNITS 21–24
Vocabulary
Exercise A

1. on
2. off
3. off
4. on
5. up

Exercise B

1. burglary, burglar, burglarize
2. shoplifting, shoplifter, shoplift
3. robbery, robber, rob
4. mugging, mugger, mug

Exercise C

1. part in
2. on
3. it easy
4. a break
5. up

Exercise D

1. laptop
2. DVD player
3. cell phone
4. digital camera
5. scanner

Grammar
Exercise A

1. Could you turn down the TV a little, please?
2. Would you mind lowering your voice, please?
3. Could you lend me some money until tomorrow, please?
4. Could I turn on the TV, please?
5. Would you take your dog inside, please?

Exercise B

1. Six cars were stolen right off the car lot.
2. The bank robber was caught as he tried to run away.
3. My new leather jacket was stolen from the backseat of my car.
4. Roberto's motorcycle was taken last night from outside his apartment.
5. Hundreds of copies of the movie were made by video pirates.

Exercise C

1. to go, going
2. working
3. to play, playing
4. washing
5. being
6. to listen, listening

Exercise D

Mr. Rodriguez,
We have a few equipment problems who that I need to bring to your attention. First, we are having problems with our printer. The technician which who/that usually does our repairs says he is behind schedule. We need someone where who/that can fix it as soon as possible. Our other problem is the scanner where which/that we use to make our brochures. It isn't working right, either. If you have someone in your department who you can send over, we would appreciate it. Finally, do you know a good place which where we can buy an inexpensive digital camera? If there is someone in your office where who/that is an expert, let us know.

Regards,
T. Withering

UNITS 25–28
Vocabulary
Exercise A

1. groom
2. best man
3. bride
4. bridesmaids
5. maid of honor
6. groomsmen

Exercise B

1. in the black
2. pay back
3. lend
4. deposit
5. save

Exercise C

1. spend
2. save
3. use
4. waste
5. spend

Exercise D

1. DJ
2. wedding
3. graduation
4. anniversary
5. family reunion

Grammar
Exercise A

1. It's not a good idea for him to ignore his family's advice.
2. It's important to her to marry someone from the same country.
3. It's important for him to finish school before he gets married.
4. It's crazy for couples to get married right after they meet.
5. It's a good idea to listen to your parents' opinions.
6. It's important for couples to discuss financial obligations before getting married.

Exercise B

1. Would you mind lending five dollars to me?
2. Could you please send a copy of your last bank statement to us?
3. We now offer all full-time employees direct deposit.
4. The sales associate forgot to give me a receipt.
5. Have you bought a wedding present for them yet?
6. The bank lent our family the money to start a new business.

Exercise C

1. You should turn down your heat at night.
2. You ought to use fluorescent light bulbs in busy areas like the kitchen or bathroom.
3. You could put your computer on "sleep mode" when you aren't using it.
4. You ought to set your thermostat for your heat or air conditioning on a timer.
5. You could use solar-powered lights outside your home.
6. In the summer, you should use curtains or shades to keep out the sunlight.

Exercise D

1. If he had a car, he would drive to work.
2. If he won the lottery, he would have a huge party.
3. If he had a private airplane, he would take trips on the weekend.
4. If he got a better job, he would move to a nicer apartment.
5. If he had a lot of money, he would buy a race car.
6. If he had a beach house, he would invite friends to visit.

WorldView 3 Student Audio CD (This CD is in your *WorldView Student Book*.)

TRACK	WORKBOOK PAGE	ACTIVITY	
1			Audio Program Introduction
2	14	Unit 1	Listening
3	14	Unit 1	Pronunciation
4	17	Unit 2	Reading/Listening
5		Unit 2	Pronunciation
6	20	Unit 3	Listening
7	20	Unit 3	Pronunciation
8		Unit 3	Pronunciation
9	20	Unit 3	Pronunciation
10	23	Unit 4	Reading/Listening
11	23	Unit 4	Pronunciation
12	28	Unit 5	Listening
13	28	Unit 5	Pronunciation
14		Unit 5	Pronunciation
15		Unit 6	Pronunciation
16	31	Unit 6	Listening
17	34	Unit 7	Pronunciation
18	34	Unit 7	Pronunciation
19	34	Unit 7	Reading/Listening
20	37	Unit 8	Reading/Listening
21		Unit 8	Pronunciation
22	42	Unit 9	Listening
23	42	Unit 9	Pronunciation
24	45	Unit 10	Listening
25	45	Unit 10	Pronunciation
26	45	Unit 10	Pronunciation
27		Unit 11	Pronunciation
28	48	Unit 11	Listening
29	51	Unit 12	Pronunciation
30	51	Unit 12	Listening
31	56	Unit 13	Reading/Listening
32		Unit 13	Pronunciation
33	59	Unit 14	Listening
34	59	Unit 14	Pronunciation
35	62	Unit 15	Reading/Listening
36		Unit 15	Pronunciation
37	65	Unit 16	Listening
38	65	Unit 16	Pronunciation
39	70	Unit 17	Reading/Listening
40	70	Unit 17	Pronunciation
41	73	Unit 18	Listening
42		Unit 18	Pronunciation
43	76	Unit 19	Listening
44	76	Unit 19	Pronunciation
45	76	Unit 19	Pronunciation
46	79	Unit 20	Pronunciation
47	79	Unit 20	Listening
48	84	Unit 21	Reading/Listening
49	84	Unit 21	Pronunciation
50	87	Unit 22	Listening
51	87	Unit 22	Pronunciation
52	90	Unit 23	Listening
53	90	Unit 23	Pronunciation
54	93	Unit 24	Pronunciation
55	93	Unit 24	Reading/Listening
56		Unit 25	Pronunciation
57	98	Unit 25	Listening
58	101	Unit 26	Reading/Listening
59	101	Unit 26	Pronunciation
60	104	Unit 27	Listening
61	104	Unit 27	Pronunciation
62	107	Unit 28	Reading/Listening
63	107	Unit 28	Pronunciation
64	17	Unit 2	Extra Pronunciation Practice
65	28	Unit 5	Extra Pronunciation Practice
66	31	Unit 6	Extra Pronunciation Practice
67	37	Unit 8	Extra Pronunciation Practice
68	48	Unit 11	Extra Pronunciation Practice
69	48	Unit 11	Extra Pronunciation Practice
70	56	Unit 13	Extra Pronunciation Practice
71	62	Unit 15	Extra Pronunciation Practice
72	73	Unit 18	Extra Pronunciation Practice
73	98	Unit 25	Extra Pronunciation Practice